D0918714

BY DANIEL J. SIEGEL, M.D., AND TINA PAYNE BRYSON, PH.D.

The Whole-Brain Child

No-Drama Discipline

The Yes Brain

The Power of Showing Up

The
Power
of Showing
Up

The Power of Showing Up

HOW PARENTAL PRESENCE
SHAPES WHO OUR KIDS
BECOME AND HOW THEIR
BRAINS GET WIRED

Daniel J. Siegel, M.D.

Tina Payne Bryson, Ph.D.

 *Ballantine Books New York*

Copyright © 2020 by Mind Your Brain, Inc., and Tina Payne Bryson, Inc.

Published in the United States by Ballantine Books, an imprint of Random House, a division of Penguin Random House LLC, New York.

BALLANTINE and the HOUSE colophon are registered trademarks of Penguin Random House LLC.

Illustrations by Tuesday Mourning

Hardback ISBN 978-1-5247-9771-3
Ebook ISBN 978-1-5247-9772-0

Printed in the United States of America on acid-free paper

randomhousebooks.com

9 8 7 6 5 4 3 2 1

First Edition

Series book design by Liz Cosgrove

DJS: For Alex and Maddi, who inspire me each day to show up as their dad even as they are out and about in the world on the journey of life we continue to share; and to Caroline, for how we continue to show up for each other. Thank you all.

TPB: For Scott, who shows up for me, and for my three "attachlings," Ben, Luke, and JP: May you find deep joy and meaning in showing up for others, and being surrounded by people who show up for you.

From Tina and Dan: For the parents and children of the world—you are our hope for the future and our bridge to showing up for Earth.

If ever there is tomorrow when we're not together . . .
there is something you must always remember.
You are braver than you believe, stronger than you seem,
and smarter than you think. But the most important thing is,
even if we're apart . . . I'll always be with you.

—Christopher Robin to Winnie-the-Pooh,
Pooh's Grand Adventure

CONTENTS

WELCOME

In our most recent book, *The Yes Brain*, we answered a question we receive from parents all the time: *What are the most important characteristics I should emphasize in my kids?* In that book we discussed the primary attributes parents should aim to instill in their children in order to help them grow into adults who live happy, successful, relational, and meaningful lives.

The book you're now holding answers a different question, one focused less on the qualities within children, and more on a parent's approach to child-rearing: *What's the single most important thing I can do for my kids to help them succeed and feel at home in the world?* Notice that this question focuses less on which skills and abilities you want to build in *your children*, and more on how *you* approach the parent-child relationship.

Our answer is simple (but not necessarily easy): Show up for your kids.

We're excited to explain what we mean by that, and to help you see how crucial the act of showing up is. We can't wait to strip away all of the child-rearing debates and controversies, and boil parenting down to the one concept that matters most when it comes to helping your kids be happy and healthy, so they enjoy and succeed in life and in relationships. We always try to avoid simplistic formulas or so-called magic bullets that offer the "one true way" to raise kids. The fact is that parenting is complex and challenging, and the answers to most questions depend on the age and stage of the child, the overall situation, and your child's temperament, not to mention your own.

We can't wait to strip away all of the child-rearing debates and controversies, and boil parenting down to the one concept that matters most when it comes to helping your kids be happy and healthy, so they enjoy and succeed in life and in relationships.

That being said, virtually all parenting questions and dilemmas do come down to the idea of relationship, so that's what we'll be focusing on here. Those of you who know our other books—*The Whole-Brain Child*, *No-Drama Discipline*, and *The Yes Brain*— will see that this book in many ways completes our quartet of titles, pulling together the various whole-brain ideas and encapsulating "what it's all about." And if you haven't read the other books yet, *The Power of Showing Up* can serve as an excellent introduction to all we've been writing about over the last several years.

Thanks for giving us the opportunity to introduce you to the importance of showing up.

Dan and Tina

The
Power of
Showing
Up

CHAPTER 1

What It Means to Show Up

One message we deliver over and over whenever we write about parenting is that you don't have to be perfect. Nobody is. There's no such thing as flawless child-rearing. (We'll pause while you let out a deep, relieved breath.) So raise a warm, left-in-the-minivan juice box to all of us imperfect parents out there.

At some level we all know this, but many of us—especially committed, thoughtful, intentional parents—consistently fall prey to feelings of anxiety or inadequacy. We worry about our children and their safety, of course, but we also worry that we're not being "good enough" in the way we're raising them. We worry that our kids won't grow up to be responsible or resilient or relational or . . . (fill in the blank). We worry about the times we let them down, or hurt them. We worry that we're not giving them enough attention, or that we're giving them *too much* attention. We even worry that we worry too much!

We've written this book for all the imperfect parents who care deeply about their kids (as well as for imperfect grandparents and teachers and professionals and anyone else who cares for a child). We have one central message full of comfort and hope: When you're not sure how to respond in a given situation with your child, don't worry.

There's one thing you can always do, and it's the best thing of all. Instead of worrying, or trying to attain some standard of perfection that simply doesn't exist, just *show up*.

Showing up means what it sounds like. It means being there for your kids. It means being *physically present,* as well as providing a *quality* of presence. Provide it when you're meeting their needs; when you're expressing your love to them; when you're disciplining them; when you're laughing together; even when you're arguing with them. You don't have to be perfect. You don't have to read all the parenting bestsellers, or sign your kids up for all the right enrichment activities. You don't have to have a committed co-parent. You don't even have to know exactly what you're doing. Just show up.

Showing up means bringing your whole being—your attention and awareness—when you're with your child. When we show up, we are mentally and emotionally present for our child in that moment. In many ways, there is no other time but now—this present moment of time—and you are in charge of learning how to show up in ways that will both greatly empower you as a parent and promote resilience and strength in your child. It's this power of presence that enables us to create an empowered mind for our children—even if we mess up on a regular basis.

Depending on your background and what kind of parents you had as a child, showing up for your own kids might come naturally. Or, you might find it difficult. You might even recognize at this moment that you're *not* showing up for your kids in a consistent way, either physically or emotionally. In the coming pages we'll discuss how, regardless of your own childhood experiences, you can be—and continue to become—the kind of parent you want to be.

Of course we all make better and worse decisions as parents, and there are all kinds of skills we can attain to help our children develop in optimal ways. But when you get right down to it, parenting is about simply being present for our kids. As we'll soon explain, the longitudinal research on child development clearly demonstrates that one of the very best predictors for how any child turns out—in terms of happiness, social and emotional development, leadership skills, meaningful relationships, and even academic and career success—is whether they developed security from having at least one person who showed up for them. Across cultures around the globe, these studies reveal a universal finding about how we can parent well, if not flawlessly.

The longitudinal research on child development clearly demonstrates that one of the very best predictors for how any child turns out—in terms of happiness, social and emotional development, leadership skills, meaningful relationships, and even academic and career success—is whether they developed security from having at least one person who showed up for them. Across cultures around the globe, these studies reveal a universal finding about how we can parent well, if not flawlessly.

And the great news is that these empirical findings can be synthesized and then made accessible for all of us imperfect parents all over the world. That's what this book is about.

What Showing Up Looks Like: The Four S's

When a caregiver predictably (not perfectly) cares for a child, that child will enjoy the very best outcomes, even in the face of significant adversity. Predictable care that supports a healthy and empowering relationship embodies what we call the "Four S's"—helping kids feel (1) *safe*—they feel protected and sheltered from harm; (2) *seen*—they know you care about them and pay attention to them; (3) *soothed*—they know you'll be there for them when they're hurting; and (4) *secure*—based on the other S's, they trust you to predictably help them feel "at home" in the world, then learn to help *themselves* feel safe, seen, and soothed.

When we can offer kids the Four S's, making repairs whenever the inevitable ruptures in these connections with our children may occur, we help create what's called "secure attachment," and it's absolutely key to optimal healthy development.

afe

een

oothed

ecure

As in our other books, everything we present here is backed by science and research. And as we'll soon explain, these ideas emerge from the field of attachment science, where for the last half century researchers have been conducting careful studies. If you know our earlier work—from Dan's title with Mary Hartzell called *Parenting from the Inside Out* and through our books *The Whole-Brain Child*, *No-Drama Discipline*, and *The Yes Brain*—then you'll immediately see, as you read the coming pages, how this book expands on what we've written before by going deeper into concepts vital to understanding the science behind whole-brain parenting. We've even added a few new twists here and there, since our understanding of parenting and the brain, along with the field of attachment science in general, continues to grow and evolve. So readers who know our work well will both see something new and feel right at home, recognizing familiar concepts while also gaining a richer understanding of them. We've worked hard to make the scientific information as accessible as possible, so that even someone approaching these ideas for the first time can follow along and immediately apply them in their personal and parenting lives.

In addition to attachment science, the other primary scientific framework underpinning our work is interpersonal neurobiology (IPNB), an approach in which we combine various fields of science into one perspective on what the mind and mental thriving are all about. IPNB looks at how our mind—including our feelings and thoughts, our attention and awareness—and our brain and the whole body are deeply interwoven within our relationships with one another and the world around us to shape who we are. The field of IPNB has dozens of professional textbooks (now over seventy) exploring the science of mental health and human development. Within those fields synthesized by IPNB is the study of attachment as well as scholarship on the brain, including a focus on how the brain changes in response to experience, called neuroplasticity.

Neuroplasticity explains how the actual physical architecture of the brain adapts to new experiences and information, reorganizing itself and creating new neural pathways based on what a person sees, hears, touches, thinks about, practices, and so on. Anything we give attention to, anything we emphasize in our experiences and interactions, creates new links in the brain. Where attention goes, neurons fire. And where neurons fire, they wire, or join together.

What does this have to do with showing up? Well, your reliable presence in the lives of your children can significantly impact the physical architecture and connectivity in their brains, creating men-

NEURONS THAT FIRE TOGETHER WIRE TOGETHER

tal models and expectations about the way the world works. A mental model is a summary the brain makes that creates a generalization of many repeated experiences. Such mental models are constructed from the past, filter our current experience, and shape how we anticipate and sometimes even sculpt our future interactions. The mental models are formed within the architecture of neural networks underlying attachment and memory.

No kidding—the experiences you provide in terms of your relationship with your child will literally mold the physical structure of her brain. Those connections in the brain in turn influence how her mind will work. In other words, when parents consistently show up, their children's minds come to expect that the world is a place that can be understood and meaningfully interacted with—even in times of trouble and pain—because the experiences you provide shape the ways the brain processes information. The brain learns to anticipate certain realities, based on what has happened before. That means your children will predict what's coming next based on previous experience. So when you are present for them, they come to expect positive interactions—from others, and from themselves. Kids learn who they are and who they can and should be, in both good times and bad, through their interactions with us, their parents. Showing up thus creates in our kids neural pathways that lead to selfhood, grit, strength, and resilience.

In doing so, it offers children the opportunity to be not only happier and more fulfilled, but more successful emotionally, relationally, and even academically. Then parenting becomes much easier as well, since children are better balanced emotionally and handle themselves better when things don't go their way.

> When parents consistently show up, their children's minds come to expect that the world is a place that can be understood and meaningfully interacted with—even in times of trouble and pain. Showing up thus creates in our kids neural pathways that lead to selfhood, grit, strength, and resilience.

Introducing the Four S's

We explain the Four S's in detail in the coming chapters, but first, here's a general idea of where we're headed. All four S's dovetail or overlap at times, because when kids feel safe, seen, and soothed, they will develop a secure attachment to their caregivers. That secure attachment is the outcome all caring parents are striving to help create in their children's lives. A securely attached relationship enables a child to feel at home in the world and to interact with others as an authentic individual who knows who she is. She approaches the world from what we've called a *Yes Brain*, interacting with new opportunities and challenges from a position of openness, curiosity, and receptiveness, rather than rigidity, fear, and reactivity. Her whole

brain is more integrated—which means she can employ the more sophisticated functions of her brain even when confronted by difficult
situations, and respond to her world from a position of security,
demonstrating more emotional balance, more resilience, more insight, and more empathy. That's what we mean when we talk about a
"whole-brain child." As a result, the child will not only be happier,
but also much more socially adept, which means she'll be better able
to get along with others, collaboratively solve problems, consider
consequences, think about other people's feelings, and on and on. In
short, a securely attached child is not only happier and more content,
but also much easier to be with and to parent.

For example, think about the first "S." An absolute requirement
for feeling secure is to feel *safe*. Kids feel safe when they feel protected
physically, emotionally, and relationally. This is the first step toward a
secure attachment, since a parent's first job is to keep his or her kids
safe. They need to *feel* and *know* that they're safe. They have to believe
that their parents are going to protect them from physical harm, but
that, also, their parents are going to keep them safe emotionally and
relationally. This doesn't mean that parents can't ever make a mistake
or say or do something that leads to hurt feelings. We're all going to
do that, a lot more than we'd like. But when we mess up with our
kids—or when they mess up with us—we repair the damage as soon
as we can.

This is how they learn that even when mistakes are made and
harsh words spoken, we still love each other and want to make things
right again. That message, when consistently delivered, leads to a
feeling of safety. Remember, the key is repair, repair, repair. There's
no such thing as perfect parenting.

The second of the Four S's focuses on helping kids feel *seen*. A big
part of parenting is about simply showing up for our kids physically:
We attend their recitals, spend time with them, play with them, read
together, and plenty more. "Quantity time" does matter, yes. Of
course it does. But *seeing* a child is more than just being physically
present. It's about attuning to what's going on inside of them and

really focusing our attention on their inner feelings, thoughts, memories—whatever is happening in their minds *beneath* their behaviors. Truly seeing a child means we pay attention to their emotions, both positive and negative. Not every second of every day; no one can do that. But on a consistent basis, we celebrate our kids' joys and victories, and we hurt with them when they experience the injuries life will inevitably deliver. We tune in to their internal landscape. That's what it means to show up emotionally and relationally, to be there for our kids and teach them what it means to love and care for someone. This is how our children come to "feel felt" by us, to sense that we feel what is going on inside them beyond just observing their external behavior. When they know that we'll dependably show up— not perfectly, and maybe not every single time—then they'll build those mental models that lead to deep security.

Research has demonstrated that when we see our child's mind, our child will learn to see his own mind as well. We call this ability

The Math of Being Seen

+

=

"mindsight" (as we'll soon discuss), and it's at the heart of emotional and social intelligence. The great news is that even if you haven't had mindsight in your own life, you can learn to develop it as an adult, and then offer mindsight conversations to your child—which we'll teach you how to do—so that he can absorb what you never had a chance to learn when you were young. Now that's a gift that can reorient your family's way of interacting toward the good, for good.

When your child feels seen by you and learns to know his own mind from these mindsight connections, he can come to understand others well, too. Add this experience of feeling seen to feeling safe, and a child will be well on the way to living a life full of security, meaning, and joy.

In addition to feeling safe and seen, we want our children to feel *soothed* during their toughest times. That doesn't mean—at all—that we rescue them from all pain and discomfort. Difficult moments are, of course, where they often learn and grow the most. We must allow our kids, depending on their age and stage of life, to experience those trying times when conflict arises with friends, teachers, and others. To put it differently, soothing our children isn't about getting rid of the waves they will inevitably face in life's ocean. It's about teaching them to ride the waves when they come—and being with them when they need us. There should never be any doubt in their minds about whether we will show up during hard times. They should know, at their core, that when they are hurting, and even when they're at their worst, we will be there. We have to let them learn that with life comes pain, but that lesson should be accompanied by the deep awareness that they'll never have to suffer alone.

Kids should know, at their core, that when they are hurting, and even when they're at their worst, we will be there. We have to let them learn that with life comes pain, but that lesson should be accompanied by the deep awareness that they'll never have to suffer alone.

Feeling safe, seen, and soothed leads to the fourth S, *security*, which is based on predictability. Again, it's not about perfection. No one can parent without making mistakes. Rather, it's about letting your kids know that they can count on you, time and again, to show up. Their security will come when they believe that you'll do all you can to keep them safe, that you'll work hard to help them feel seen when they come to you, and that when things don't go their way, you'll be there to soothe them. The neurobiological effect of the Four S's is an integrated brain: a nervous system that's resilient and that doesn't stay in prolonged stress. As a result, kids can approach life

The neurobiological effect of the Four S's is an integrated brain: a nervous system that's resilient and that doesn't stay in prolonged stress. As a result, kids can approach life from an assumption that they are safe, that love and relationships will be consistent and present in their lives, and that they can handle life's inevitable difficult moments, leaving them feeling secure and at home in the world.

from an assumption that they are safe, that love and relationships will be consistent and present in their lives, and that they can handle life's inevitable difficult moments, leaving them feeling secure and at home in the world.

Secure Attachment: The Ultimate Goal

You can see the power behind showing up, so that kids feel consistently safe, seen, soothed, and secure. But let us be clear: Showing up isn't the goal of parenting. Rather, it's the *means* by which you move toward your desired outcome. The actual goal is what's called secure attachment. That's what we want for our kids. There's nothing more important we can do for them. Secure attachment increases children's lifelong satisfaction and happiness. Moreover, it optimizes their sense of identity, the quality of their relationships, their academic and career success, and even how their brains develop.

Let's get more specific. Study after study has proven that kids who are securely attached are more likely to develop a huge number of benefits, listed opposite.

Take a moment and look at this list. When we talk about secure attachment as the ultimate goal of parenting, these characteristics are in large part why. Put simply, when kids are securely attached to their caregivers, they have a much greater opportunity to thrive—in school, in relationships, and in life.

And how do you develop that secure attachment in your kids? That's right. By showing up. Scientific studies have repeatedly shown that one of the single best predictors for how any child turns out—in measure after measure—is that they had at least one person who was emotionally attuned and present for them—what we are simply calling having someone "show up" for them. It's all pretty simple (but again, not always easy): To give your kids the best chance for healthy and optimal development, all you have to do is help them feel safe, seen, soothed, and secure. And to do that, you just need to be there for them—to be present—which means being receptive to who they

the BENEFITS of a SECURE ATTACHMENT

- HIGHER SELF-ESTEEM

- BETTER EMOTIONAL REGULATION

- GREATER ACADEMIC SUCCESS

- BETTER COPING IN TIMES OF STRESS

- MORE POSITIVE ENGAGEMENT WITH PRESCHOOL PEERS

- CLOSER FRIENDSHIPS IN MIDDLE CHILDHOOD

- MORE EFFECTIVE SOCIAL INTERACTION IN ADOLESCENCE

- HAPPIER AND BETTER RELATIONSHIPS WITH PARENTS

- STRONGER LEADERSHIP QUALITIES

- A GREATER SENSE OF SELF-AGENCY

- MORE TRUSTING, NON-HOSTILE ROMANTIC RELATIONSHIPS IN ADULTHOOD

- MORE EMPATHY

- GREATER SOCIAL COMPETENCE OVERALL

- GREATER TRUST IN LIFE

are, giving them the experience of security. You might think of showing up as a fifth "S," guiding you to the other four.

There are several key reasons a secure attachment produces these positive outcomes. For one thing, when you show up for your kids, they feel safe and secure overall. They work from a sense of belonging in the world, so that even when things don't go their way, they know they're okay.

A good way to think about it is that secure attachment serves as a mediating factor when children face obstacles and frustrations. A secure attachment won't keep kids from experiencing negative situations and emotions. We're talking about life, after all. They're going to feel pain—not to mention disappointment, aggravation, dissatisfaction, and so on.

Your job as a parent is *not* to prevent them from experiencing setbacks and failures, but to give them the tools and emotional resilience they need to weather life's storms, and then to walk beside them through those storms.

Your job as a parent is *not* to prevent them from experiencing setbacks and failures, but to give them the tools and emotional resilience they need to weather life's storms, and then to walk beside them through those storms.

A secure attachment, then, is like emotional protective gear on par with a skateboarding helmet. Wearing a helmet won't prevent an accident, but it can lead to drastically different consequences if there is a mishap.

Similarly, a child with a secure attachment won't somehow bypass the many pains and letdowns that accompany growing up. He may still feel rejected when he doesn't get invited to a friend's birthday party. And when he gets older, he may still get his heart broken by the first person he falls in love with. But when these challenges occur, he'll have the protective emotional padding to handle the party snub with resilience, and get through the anguish of heartache without permanently losing a solid sense of self.

A secure attachment can smooth things out for kids, especially for those dealing with extra challenges like traumatic life experiences, environmental stress, developmental or medical or genetic challenges, or learning difficulties.

A secure attachment can smooth things out for kids, especially for those dealing with extra challenges like traumatic life experiences, environmental stress, developmental or medical or genetic challenges, or learning difficulties.

Without secure attachment.

Secure attachment as emotional protective gear.

A simple truth is that life can be harder for certain children, and it can feel like they are constantly pedaling a bicycle up a steep hill. You may not be able to remove the force of gravity or flatten the hill, but if you can provide the Four S's by consistently showing up, you can at least regrade the slope so that pedaling isn't quite so arduous.

For some kids life is especially hard.

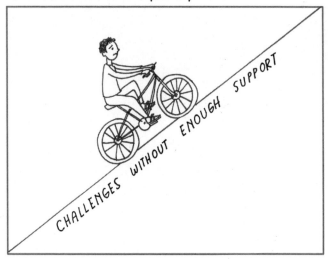

We can make it easier by showing up for them.

Again, it's not that you'll take away the many challenges your child is facing. But with your love and presence, you can smooth out the road and make it easier for him to deal with the obstacles that come up. Then, he can learn both to show up for himself and to find healthy ways to lean on others for support. When things get tough, his internal emotional resilience will help him figure out what to do.

That goes for making difficult choices as well. Research is really clear: What seem like personal, inner skills—like self-awareness and emotional resilience—are actually developed from kids' interpersonal interactions, from their relationships with their caregivers and others as they grow. Securely attached children are better able to regulate their emotions and make good decisions. They are more adept at considering consequences and the perspectives of others and at handling themselves in ways that are constructive and beneficial, rather than harmful and destructive. This of course makes things easier on both child and parent, as well as the relationship between the two.

One final reason secure attachment produces such powerful outcomes is that it gives kids what attachment researchers call a "secure base" from which to explore their world. It lets them feel free to go out and see what lies beyond the horizon. As parents, we are not just a safe haven; we are also a launching pad. We'll explain this point more fully in the coming pages. The key idea, though, is that with secure attachment, kids can approach the world from a Yes-Brain mentality. They're emotionally balanced, resilient, insightful, and empathetic. They can display all of these attributes because they feel safe and comfortable in the world, because they have a secure base at home.

Securely attached children are better able to regulate their emotions and make good decisions. They are more adept at considering consequences and the perspectives of others and at handling themselves in ways that are constructive and beneficial, rather than harmful and destructive. This of course makes things easier on both child and parent, as well as the relationship between the two.

Getting Clear on Your Own Story

To provide this secure base, and all that comes with it, we as parents will be best equipped if we come to know who we are—to be "self-aware," and to know our own history and how our own childhood has shaped how we grew up. With that truth in mind, a substantial portion of the book will be devoted to helping you comprehend your own story, and understand the type of attachment you received from your caregivers. The greatest predictor for how well parents can provide secure attachment and show up for their kids is whether they've reflected on their own experiences and the extent to which they felt the Four S's from their own caregivers.

Notice that we didn't say that parents must have been parented well themselves in order to provide secure attachment to their children. The science regarding this concept sends a strong message, one of hope and not despair—that even if we didn't have secure attachment from our own caregivers, we can still provide it to our own children, *if we've reflected on and made sense of our own attachment history*. That is exhilarating, research-established news!

We want to stress this point here: You really can provide a loving, stable foundation for your child, even if you didn't receive one from your own parents.

Even if we didn't have secure attachment from our own caregivers, we can still provide it to our own children, *if we've reflected on and made sense of our own attachment history*. You really can provide a loving, stable foundation for your child, even if you didn't receive one from your own parents.

To that end, much of this book is aimed at helping you gain as much clarity as possible regarding the way you were raised and how your relationships impacted you. When you develop what we call a "coherent narrative" about your own past, you can be much more intentional and consistent as a parent, and much more effective in the ways you show up for your kids. Therefore, beginning in the next chapter, and throughout the book, we will give you the opportunity to explore to what extent you have felt safe, seen, soothed, and secure in your own life. With this deeper knowledge about your own history and experiences, you'll be better able to provide the Four S's for your kids. That means you can show up—early and often, as they say.

Our overall message here is one of hope. Working from the latest research in IPNB, neuroplasticity, and attachment science, we want to highlight an inspirational declaration: History is not destiny. Our past can be *understood* so that it doesn't dictate our present and our future. We don't have to run from our past, nor do we have to be enslaved by it. Remember, where attention goes, neural firing flows and neural connection grows. It's never too late to make sense of your life. Doing so can transform not only your relationship with your kids, but with yourself as well, as it can actually change how your brain has been wired.

You can think of this process as a chain of events. Working backward, it goes like this: The ultimate parenting goal is secure attachment for our kids. That comes from showing up and providing the S's. To do that we need to make sense of our own individual stories, our own relational and attachment history. So that's where it all begins: with understanding the type of attachment we received from our own caregivers. The chain, then, looks like this:

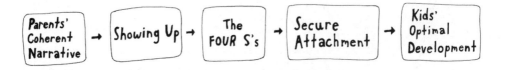

We're focusing primarily on the parent-child dynamic, but we want to emphasize one note here at the beginning: All the ideas we'll discuss in the coming chapters apply to any relationship. When we are able to show up for the people we care about, our relationships thrive, our brains are healthier and more integrated, and our lives are more meaningful.

We've Written This Book for You, Wherever You Are as a Parent

Like our previous books—*The Whole-Brain Child, No-Drama Discipline*, and *The Yes Brain*—our focus here is on children's brains, and on offering you new ways to think about how best to nurture your child's developing mind. Certain parents might approach this focus from different perspectives, and as we wrote this book we had four different types of parents in mind.

The first group is made up of those who obsess and worry that they need to *do* better and *be* better as parents. They agonize over mistakes and missed opportunities with their children. They "should" themselves to death, sometimes in the form of regrets ("I should have taught my child Spanish" or "I shouldn't have missed that first inning of the fourteenth Little League game of the season"), and sometimes in the form of worries about the future ("I should take her to volunteer at the shelter more, so she doesn't grow up to be spoiled" or "I should spend more time teaching him about empathy while we're in the car so he'll be a kinder adult"). And worst of all, they punish themselves when they make mistakes with their children, constantly telling themselves some version of "I should be better."

Sound familiar? If it does, then our message here is one of consolation: You're doing fine. You're showing up. That's what matters. You don't have to be perfect; you can't be. We are all lifelong learners. Just be there for your kids. Love them. Use discipline moments as opportunities to teach and build skills. Model kindness, respect, and self-care. Apologize when you

You're doing fine. You're showing up. That's what matters. You don't have to be perfect; you can't be. We are all lifelong learners. Just be there for your kids. Love them. Use discipline moments as opportunities to teach and build skills. Model kindness, respect, and self-care. Apologize when you miss an opportunity to connect or you mess up in other ways. They don't need every advantage, and they don't need a superparent. They just need you—authentic, flawed, and fully present you.

miss an opportunity to connect or you mess up in other ways. They don't need every advantage, and they don't need a superparent. They just need you—authentic, flawed, and fully present you. If you're one of these parents, our message is to cut yourself a bit of slack.

We're also addressing those parents who have a child who is struggling, acting out, or in crisis. These parents are simply wondering how to deal with their child, how to manage the overwhelming challenges they face every day. If you're facing similar struggles, then *showing up* will help you realize the fundamental and most important things you need to do for that child. As in our other books, we'll offer specific, practical strategies that can help a child who is crying out for love and support.

A third audience is new or expectant parents who feel completely lost and overwhelmed at the thought of guiding a young person through childhood and adolescence. If you fall into this category, the clear, practical theories and strategies we discuss will not only give you an overarching philosophy on how to approach first-time parenting, but also provide you with specific, precise steps that will help you interact with your children in loving, intentional ways. You can even think of this book as a beginner's guide to raising kids, helping you focus on what's most important in your new and exciting (and yes, often scary) journey.

And finally, we're specifically addressing the growing number of parents who are becoming less and less present in the lives of their children. Sometimes it's because of excessively long work hours and the multitude of demands on the modern family. Also, though, as screens command more and more of our time, parents are increasingly allowing their devices to claim the attention that would previously have gone to their children, drastically diminishing opportunities for parent-child interaction.

The showing up message takes this phenomenon head on—without judgment, and without blame or shame. The reality is obvious: We live in a device-filled world, and the genie is already out of the bottle. Screens are an integral and helpful part of our world, and electronics provide great advantages that all of us count on and enjoy. We're not arguing anything different. (Many of you are at this very moment reading this book on a screen, and we certainly don't have a problem with that!) But we *are* concerned when the devices prevent parents from showing up in the lives of their kids. It becomes a problem when parents are physically present, but not at all engaged—not truly *present*. So in the coming pages we offer specific ways you can take a realistic and intentional approach to spending time with your children.

Regardless of which of the above categories you fit into, we want to offer you both hope and guidance as you look for ways to be the parent you want to be, and thus help your kids grow into adults who live rich, meaningful, connected lives.

By the way, we keep talking about parents, but we're very aware that plenty of grandparents and other caregivers are helping raise children these days. Everything we say here applies to those relationships as well. In addition, we greatly admire the numerous educators and clinicians who support the work of parents and other caregivers, and we've kept these professionals in mind as we offer principles and perspectives that can guide their work as well as resources they can recommend to the troubled parents they see in their offices.

Whoever you are, and whatever has motivated you to pick up this book, please know how much we appreciate your including us on this journey toward improving the lives of the children you love. Simply by reading these pages, you're taking a huge step toward showing up. And that's what it's all about.

CHAPTER 2

Why Do Some Parents Show Up, While Others Don't?

An Introduction to Attachment Science

W *hat makes a good parent?*

Ask people this question and you'll get a range of answers. Some will focus on that person's experiences with their own parents; others on the person's knowledge level, especially in terms of parenting philosophies. Some might emphasize the parents' religious upbringing, or how moral and ethical they are—or how hard they work at being consistent, kind, patient, and so on.

All of those factors can definitely influence our parenting. But as we explained in chapter 1, decades of rigorous research provide a specific answer to this question, and it's profoundly hopeful. If we want to look at why kids do well in life (emotionally, relationally, socially, educationally, and so on), we can examine whether they've developed secure attachment with at least one caregiver who consistently shows up for them. And the best predictor for whether caregivers can provide this type of secure attachment is that they have what we can simply call "parental presence." Parents with presence have reflected on and made sense of their own story and attachment history. Even if that history was challenging, making sense of one's life empowers parents to have the open, receptive awareness of presence that enables them to show up reliably for their children.

What produces deep and lasting success for kids?

A secure attachment to a caregiver who shows up.

How do we provide that secure attachment?

First, by developing a coherent narrative that makes sense of our own early life experiences.

To restate it as simply as possible, kids are most likely to become resilient, caring, and strong when parents show up. We don't have to be perfect, but the ways in which we show up (or fail to show up) influence who our kids become and how their brains get wired.

Naturally there are other factors—random events, inborn features of temperament, inherited vulnerabilities—that we cannot change and that also influence how our children develop. But when it comes to what we *can* do to shape our kids' growth, the research is solid. Parents who show up are the ones who have made sense of their own life experiences, creating a "coherent narrative" and being able to offer parental presence so that they show up inside and out. Inside we come to understand how the *past* has shaped who we are in the *present* in a way that frees us to be what we want to be now and in the *future*. And outside, we learn how to have an open, receptive awareness—to have *parental presence*—so that our child feels felt, understood, and connected to us. Making sense and being present: That's what showing up is all about. And that's where we'll begin, with helping you consider how well you've made sense of your experiences with your own parents and how you can be present in the lives of your kids.

Making sense and being present: That's what showing up is all about. And that's where we'll begin, with helping you consider how well you've made sense of your experiences with your own parents and how you can be present in the lives of your kids.

How much have you reflected on the ways your childhood experiences influenced your own development, thus predicting and influencing the ways you interact with your children? How do you think your early family life impacted the ways your brain developed in response to those experiences, either directly or by how you had to learn to adapt, or perhaps even survive, in the face of challenging events?

How much have you reflected on the ways your childhood experiences influenced your own development, thus predicting and influencing the ways you interact with your children?

The good news is that if you're willing to do the work, science can show you how to understand your own attachment history. What's more, even if you didn't receive an optimal upbringing—because of your parents' absence, their blind spots, their mistreatment of you, or any other reason—your attachment strategy is not fixed. History is not destiny.

History is **NOT** <u>destiny</u>. By making sense of your own story, you can be the kind of parent you want to be – regardless of how you were parented.

If your parents failed to show up for you, or showed up only sometimes, or behaved in scary and damaging ways, that doesn't mean you can't be there for your own kids in healthy and constructive ways. But it *does* mean you may have some work to do in terms of reflecting on your own attachment history and determining the kind of attachment you want to provide your own children. You can actually *choose* the extent to which you show up for your kids, and yes, you can build your own capacity to show up by examining your history and making sense of it for yourself.

Basic Attachment Science: What It Means for You as a Parent

Let's begin by introducing the basics of attachment science. If you know our other work, you've already been exposed to some of the fundamentals. In the rest of this book we'll cover those essentials and add to what we've said before. The field of attachment science continues to expand as new information—from fields like evolutionary theory, genetics, and epigenetics—bolsters its fundamental tenets. In the coming pages we'll introduce new ways to think about the self and relationships, and we'll apply that information to the concepts we introduced in the previous chapter. We think you'll find it as fascinating as we do and hope that it illuminates your own experiences, both with your parents and with your children.

The knowledge we've gained from the field of attachment science over the last several decades has profoundly affected the way we understand parenting and child development. Dan received a National Institute of Mental Health research training grant to study attachment before he directed the clinical training program in child and adolescent psychiatry at UCLA, and Tina, in her research during her doctoral program and beyond, has focused on this science and its practical applications from the interpersonal neurobiology framework. The field's science is rich and reliable, and it has powerful implications for how we can apply its findings across a wide array of cultures and family situations to optimize children's development. Thankfully, the information doesn't feel nearly as unfamiliar today as it has in the recent past.

Here it is in a nutshell: Children who form strong bonds—secure attachments—with their parents at a very young age lead much happier and more fulfilling lives. These attachment bonds are formed when parents respond to the needs of their children and dependably provide comfort, as when they pick them up when they cry, or hold and reassure them when they are upset. When children experience this type of reliable behavior and connection, they are then freed to learn and develop without having to use attention or energy to survive, or to remain hypervigilant, watching for slight changes in their environment or in their caregivers.

We are all born with the innate drive to connect, and when that connection is reliably established and repairs are made in response to relational ruptures, then the brain can grow in optimal ways. When children are offered a secure attachment with their primary care-

When children are offered a secure attachment with their primary caregiver, these predictable and therefore reliable experiences reduce their levels of stress and allow them to develop confidence and ultimately self-reliance. They learn how to manage their own feelings and behaviors, enabling them to flourish and thrive.

giver, these predictable and therefore reliable experiences reduce their levels of stress and allow them to develop confidence and ultimately self-reliance. They learn how to manage their own feelings and behaviors, enabling them to flourish and thrive.

We know this may sound amazing, but it is amazingly true: We learn to become who we are and even to *know* who we are by how we experience being in connection with our attachment figure. What you may have thought was a personal and inner, private experience, like sensing your emotions and regulating them, or being aware of your memories about certain events, actually emerges from your social relationships with important others in your life. We are profoundly social creatures, and our relational connections shape our inner neural connections. The child's mind develops with this *interpersonal* shaping of the *inner personal*. (Much more about this later.) That's why a secure attachment can be so powerful in terms of affecting healthy development.

On the other hand, when this type of bonding doesn't take place, children don't learn these crucial lessons and skills, putting them at a higher risk of all kinds of problems: aggression, defiance, hyperactivity, poorer language development, weaker executive function, and even less resilience in the face of systemic problems like poverty, family instability, and parental stress and depression.

Seems logical, doesn't it? The kids who feel loved and supported, who can count on their parents to show up for them physically and emotionally, will do better in life. In fact, even if one parent fails to show up, but another caregiver does provide the kind of constancy and predictability a child needs, that child will receive many of those same benefits that come with secure attachment.

The science behind this fundamental reality is fascinating, and fairly simple to follow. We want to introduce you to some of the basics of the science and show you how powerful it can be for understanding yourself and your interactions with your kids. We'll start by looking at one groundbreaking research study that initiated a new way of understanding development. By the way, in case you're interested in taking a deeper dive into the science behind what we're discussing here, take a look at Dan's book *The Developing Mind: How Relationships and the Brain Interact to Shape Who We Are*. It's now in its third edition and reviews thousands of scientific studies supporting this and the other research findings we'll be drawing on throughout the book.

One note before we proceed: We've tried to make sure that the explanations that follow are as clear and concise as possible (while always staying true to the science), so they can be understood by any layperson. We encourage you to read the remainder of the chapter if you'd like to understand the basics of attachment science at a deeper level. However, if you're less interested in the scientific details, feel free to skip to chapter 3, where we present the more practical ramifications of all that we discuss here.

Attachment Science and the Strange Situation Experiment

In the 1960s, scientists developed a fascinating and revealing test they began giving children and their caregivers at the child's first birthday. Throughout the first year of the child's life, trained observers made home visits to assess mother-infant interactions using a standardized rating scale. Then, at the end of the year, each mother-infant pair was brought into a room for an experiment that lasted about twenty minutes. This test is known as the "Infant Strange Situation," because it focuses on what happens when babies are separated from their mothers and left in a "strange situation"—in an unfamiliar room either with strangers or alone. By looking at how one-year-olds react when dealing with the stress of watching their mothers leave a room, and especially how they respond when the mothers return, researchers found that they could learn a great deal about the babies' attachment system—the way they connect with their primary caregivers and use that relationship as a "secure base."

Over the thousands of times these studies have been repeated across many cultures, we've learned that the key to the relational assessment is the reunion phase: how the child greets the returning mother, how readily the child calms when comforted, and how quickly the child returns to playing with the toys in the room. (Later, these same experiments were performed with fathers, with the same general results—so we can say that this is an assessment of the child–caregiver relationship.) Securely attached babies—meaning that the relationship with that parent is secure—show clear signs of missing their mother when she leaves the room, actively greet her when she returns, then settle down quickly and return to their toys and activities once the mother is back in the room.

Securely attached babies—meaning that the relationship with that parent is secure—show clear signs of missing their mother when she leaves the room, actively greet her when she returns, then settle down quickly and return to their toys and activities once the mother is back in the room.

Not surprisingly, researchers find that the securely attached children are the ones whose parents, in home-visit observations, are sensitive and responsive to the baby's bid for connection, and whose parents can read their children's cues and consistently meet their needs. In other words, the caregiver receives the child's signals, makes sense of what they mean in terms of the inner experience of the child—the mind beneath the child's behavior—then responds in a predictable, timely, sensitive, and effective manner.

How common is this secure attachment? Researchers who perform the Strange Situation paradigm consistently find that about two-thirds of the children are securely attached to their primary caregivers. They don't have perfect parents (whatever that would

The Strange Situation - Reunion: Secure Attachment

Touches Base

Returns to Play

even mean), but they have parents who consistently show up for them when they need them, and this produces secure attachment.

The other third of all children exhibit what's called *insecure attachment with their primary caregiver*, and they fall into one of three groupings. One thing to keep in mind as you read the following descriptions: These groupings are about a relationship and how a child adapts to that relationship; they are *not* a measure of the child alone.

The first group of insecurely attached children, when observed in the Strange Situation, demonstrate what's called an *avoidant attachment*. When their mother leaves them alone, they focus most intently on the toys in the room. In fact, they show practically no external distress or anger when their mother departs, and they ignore or even avoid her when she returns.

As you might suspect, home observations of avoidantly attached children show that the parents seem indifferent or insensitive to the children's signals and needs. They meet their children's *physical* needs and provide them with toys and activities, but *emotional* needs are ignored. As a result, even when the children are experiencing internal physiological distress, they learn the skill of minimizing their externally expressed needs for attachment. The need to have one's inner state, or emotions, felt and soothed by the caregiver seems to "go underground." In other words, the baby adapts to not having his basic human relational needs met. Even signs of distress are dismissed in interacting with a parent with whom the child has developed an avoidant attachment, leaving the child to surmise that the parent isn't interested in his distress, and that he'll either get a better response or simply won't waste energy and experience frustration if he just doesn't show that he is upset. Essentially, these children adapt to this kind of relationship with what's called behavioral avoidance—they cope with their parent's lack of attunement by saying, in effect, that they don't care whether the mother is in the room or not.

A child can be avoidantly attached to one parent, but still enjoy secure attachment, along with the benefits that come with it, with another caregiver.

By the way, in case you're wondering, this attachment strategy is specific to the relational history of interactions with that specific parent, and can be quite independent when assessed with other caregivers. That's right—a child can be avoidantly attached to one parent, but still enjoy secure attachment, along with the benefits that come with it, with another caregiver.

The Strange Situation - Reunion: Avoidant Attachment

Ignores Parent

Continues to Play

The second group of children with insecure attachment fall into what's called *ambivalent attachment*. Here the parents show their children neither consistent nurturing and attunement nor consistent indifference and insensitivity. Instead, what characterizes the early years of life for these children is parental inconsistency. They have a parent who is sometimes attuned, sensitive, and responsive, and at other times not. As a result, the attachment relationship causes this

The Strange Situation - Reunion: Ambivalent Attachment

Does Not Become Settled, Even in Parent's Arms

Does Not Easily Return to Play

child great anxiety and ambivalence regarding whether they can trust this parent.

In the Strange Situation, for example, the ambivalently attached infant is inconsolable both when his mother leaves *and* when she returns. Instead of returning to the toys as a securely attached child would, he clings to his parent with concern or even desperation.

The Strange Situation - Reunion: Disorganized Attachment

Approaches Parent

Avoids Reconnecting

There appears to be a lack of trust that the relationship will provide reliable nurturance and soothing, and as a result, even physical contact with the mother fails to give the child a sense of relief.

The history of inconsistency creates an internal sense of confusion, and the presence of the parent upon return seems to activate this anxious and uncertain state. Whereas the avoidantly attached child discussed above focuses away from the relationship and often exclusively on the toys, thus minimizing the activation of the attachment system and its bids for connection, the ambivalently attached child is afraid to move his attention away from his mother for fear that she might leave while he's not looking, and in this way can be seen to maximize the attachment system.

The third and most distressed type of insecure attachment is *disorganized attachment,* where a child has trouble deciding how to respond when the mother returns to the room, and as a result demonstrates disorganized, disoriented, or chaotic behavior. The child might appear terrified, then approach the mother, then withdraw, then fall on the floor helpless and cry, then freeze up. The child may even cling to the mother while simultaneously pulling away.

Disorganized attachment results when children find their parents *severely* unattuned, when the parents are frightening, and/or when the parents themselves are frightened. Unlike the children in the other types of attachment, who develop organized patterns—secure or insecure—for responding to and dealing with a sensitive, disconnected, or inconsistent caregiver, here the child has trouble coming up with any consistent or effective way to cope with distress induced by a caregiver who at times causes terror in the child.

What Do Childhood Attachment Patterns Have to Do with How We Parent?

Many of the children who took part in the initial Infant Strange Situation experiments have been followed over the last third of a century and longer. That's pretty amazing, isn't it? The children who were studied as infants are now adults, many with their own children. That means that, based on longitudinal follow-up research, we can see how those participants' childhood experiences have impacted their relational tendencies as adults. Researchers have been intrigued to discover that despite all of the influences and experiences in the lives of the children as they grew up, the vast majority of kids remained in the same attachment categories—secure, insecure-avoidant, insecure-ambivalent, or insecure-disorganized—even into adulthood. Those that have changed often had changes in their relational worlds that helped them understand the changes in their attachment.

Attachment scientists have developed names for the adult attachment patterns that correspond to these childhood patterns. As we discuss each of them, see which one most closely resembles your own experiences. Think about your own attachment history from childhood, and how it has played out as you've become an adult. You can also use this information to better understand your partner, as well as your friends. You might even keep it in mind as you choose your babysitters and other caregivers, and possibly even your children's schools if you have that option.

One important note to keep in mind as you read about these categories: Most of us have different facets of the various attachment patterns within us to some extent. You might identify parts of yourself in one category, then recognize that you also fit into a different pattern as well. People typically don't fit neatly and discretely into only one category. But most likely, you'll find yourself identifying with one attachment pattern over the others as you read the following descriptions.

People typically don't fit neatly and discretely into only one category. But most likely, you'll find yourself identifying with one attachment pattern over the others.

Secure and Free Attachment

Certain kids are fortunate enough to become adults who generally enjoy good relationships, feel respected by their peers, meet their intellectual potential, and regulate their emotions well. Attachment researchers have called this adult version of secure attachment *free attachment*. Because of the consistent love and attention they were shown as children, these individuals became adults with an unconstrained and self-directed autonomy where they felt free to look at and understand their past, free to be themselves in the present, and free to follow their dreams and desires in the future. In this way, a pattern of adaptation to an attachment relationship becomes a way that the individual learns to regulate her emotions, thinking, memory, self-awareness, and capacity for mutually rewarding interpersonal relationships. The science is quite clear: We develop emotional and social intelligence through the security of our attachment relationships.

Children with secure relational patterns have their bids for connection met with sensitivity, and repair is made when ruptures inevitably arise. Their needs are perceived, made sense of, and responded to. Their parents show up for them. At four months old, for instance, a baby might cry. Her father hears her, leaves whatever he's doing, and picks her up, asking, "Hungry?" Then he tenderly feeds her.

Her signals of distress have been perceived and attended to. He made sense of what she needed and responded to her effectively in a timely and caring fashion. Children fortunate enough to have such

Attuned parenting leads to secure attachment.

attentive parents feel connected and protected, especially during times of emotional need, which produces feelings of safety and a secure base from which to explore the world.

Is it any wonder, then, that such children grow into adults who, because of their secure attachment history, can go through life much more smoothly, overcoming its many challenges and disappointments and embracing and enjoying the beautiful moments? These adults value relationships, communicating well and demonstrating empathy for others, but they also remain independent and self-sufficient. They are resilient in the face of stress and can regulate their emotions and bodies, and they show insight into their own mind and behavior. As a result, they are willing and able to show up when their own kids need them, just as the father did for his hungry four-month-old.

To help you keep track of the various terms we introduce in this chapter, we'll construct a chart along the way, adding to it with each new term.

Child Attachment Pattern	Parenting Tendencies	Child's Wired Assumptions
Secure	*Secure* attachment pattern: Sensitive, attuned, responsive to baby's bid for connection; an ability to read child's cues and predictably meet child's needs. Parent reliably "shows up" for child.	My parent isn't perfect, but I know I'm safe. If I have a need she will see it and respond quickly and sensitively. I can trust that other people will do that, too. My inner experience is real and worthy of being expressed and respected.
Insecure: Avoidant		
Insecure: Ambivalent		
Insecure: Disorganized		

Avoidant and Dismissing Attachment

Obviously, not everyone is born into a family that affords them secure attachment experiences. Children with one of the three insecure
attachment patterns typically grow up to develop relationships that,
to some degree, are characterized by chaos, rigidity, or both.

The children with the first type of insecure attachment, avoidant
attachment, tend to grow up to be adults who have difficulty connecting not only with others, but also with their internal landscape.
They are often unaware of or unwilling to deal with emotions, and
they have difficulty connecting with the minds and emotions of others they are in relationship with. They rigidly avoid dealing with the
past, their emotions, and relational closeness. And this makes sense
based on their childhood experiences. As kids their emotional needs
were largely ignored, so learning to dismiss their feelings was simply
a survival strategy, the basis for a learned attachment pattern.

Imagine a different scenario for the four-month-old mentioned
above. This time she cries, but her father doesn't notice for a while as
he simply dismisses her calls and continues reading his book. Then,
when he finally does respond, he's irritated at being interrupted. In
his frustration he changes her diaper and angrily puts her back in her
playpen, but she continues fussing. Further exasperated, he moves
her to her crib, thinking she must be tired. She continues to cry and
fuss, and eventually, after an hour of hunger, he finally gives her a
bottle.

What does the baby learn from repeated interactions like this,
where her father's response to her cries is so delayed and out of touch
with what she's actually feeling and needing at that moment? That
her father doesn't read her signals very well. That he doesn't hear or
understand her. When he consistently fails to pay attention to her
communication cues, she learns, correctly, that her dad isn't available
to meet her needs or connect with her emotionally. Over time she
may experience that there's no one to really *get* her on a deep level,
that her parent will not see her mind, and that she cannot count on

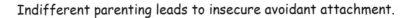

Indifferent parenting leads to insecure avoidant attachment.

others to be interested in her needs and emotions. Eventually, in order to adapt in her environment, and to get the best response from her caregiver, she will also become wired to avoid and dismiss emotions and the importance of relationships. In other words, relationships were not helpful in the past, so why would she rely on them in any significant way in the future?

Indulge us for a moment as we explain some of the neuroscience behind how a child's brain might adapt like this and learn to deny emotions. In our other work we've explained that you can think of the brain as a house with an upstairs and a downstairs, each of which is tasked with different capabilities and responsibilities. The downstairs brain is made up of the brain stem and the physically lower parts of the brain, including the limbic system, which controls emotions and drives. That downstairs brain is the origin for our more primitive and instinctual processes, like basic bodily functions, innate impulses, and strong feelings. The upstairs brain, in contrast, is made up of the prefrontal cortex and the other higher parts of the brain. It's the more evolved part of the brain and is responsible for higher-order thinking having to do with tasks like imagination, decision-making, empathy, personal insight, and morality.

So one way to explain how learning shapes the brain is that the child's inner needs for connection—which reside in the more primitive downstairs brain—remain so unmet because of avoidant attachment that the brain learns to shut down those inner signals from entering awareness in the upstairs brain. As a defense measure, the signals about those basic needs get rejected and blocked from reaching the upstairs brain. It turns out that most of the body's signals, and even many of those from the downstairs limbic and brain stem areas, first arrive in the right side of the cortex. Amazingly, as you may have heard, the right and left sides of the brain are quite different in many ways—the timing of their development (right first), their structure (right more interconnected within itself), and their functions (right has a broad, wide attentional focus whereas the left has a narrow

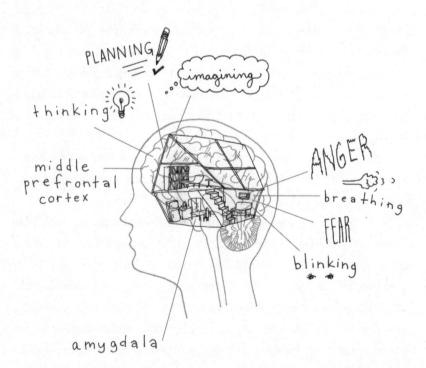

focus; the right receives input from the lower areas, including the body, whereas the left tends to specialize in linguistic symbols—our spoken and written language).

With this setup, imagine this: If you could shut down your awareness of the downstairs brain and the body's input to the cortex where consciousness in part arises, then you would not be so distressed by your parent's missing your signals for connection. This could be achieved by simply developing the left cortex activity and disconnecting it from the right—so that as you developed, you'd be unaware of your internal bodily states as well as the internal sensations of longing and disappointment that are processed by your heart and your gut. You'd literally be shutting yourself off from your own internal world.

One important piece of research data—one that applies both to children with avoidant attachment relationships and to what we'll soon discuss as the dismissing attachment of their parents—is that when these subjects are faced with issues related to attachment, their physiology shows significant signs of distress even though their external behaviors convey a nonchalant attitude. For the Infant Strange Situation, this looks like an infant who doesn't go toward the mother, even though his psychometric data (like heart rate) reveals stress at the time of the parent's return. His downstairs brain and his body *know* that relationships are important, and the timing of the stress reaction illuminates that the need for connection remains, even if the learned strategy of attachment is to minimize the attachment system's external activation in the form of behavior.

Briefly, three systems in the brain are involved in how attachment influences our deepest networks. One is the reward system that extends from the downstairs to the upstairs brain. Attachment is rewarding. The second is the system that senses and regulates the body—and thus is fundamental to our sense of survival. The third is sometimes called the "mentalizing" network, meaning how we sense the mind of our caregivers and ultimately of ourselves with what we simply call mindsight. Reward, bodily regulation, and mindsight are three distinct networks in the brain that are woven together by attachment relationships in both childhood and our adult lives.

Let's look at how these systems play out from the lens of avoidant attachment.

When those with avoidant attachment are in a situation that activates their attachment networks, in order to maintain bodily regulation with their history of non-connecting relational experiences with this caregiver, they shut off their reward circuit drive for connection in this moment. But what is also shut off is the mindsight network that would perceive the mental state of their caregiver, and perhaps even of themselves. It turns out that seeing the mind and regulating the body each have a right-sided dominance in the brain. We can make sense of these findings then with the proposal of a left-dominant way of living in the world among individuals with this avoidant attachment history. One result of this adaptive neural strategy of survival is that the sensitivity to nonverbal signals—eye contact, facial expressions including tears, tone of voice such as distress or anger, posture, gestures, and the timing and intensity of responses—is reduced in adults with a dismissing pattern of attachment—those who've likely had avoidant attachment histories in their childhood. In addition, one of the hallmarks of the narratives of these individuals is to state, repeatedly, that they don't recall their childhood experiences. And this is true not just for young childhood (before the age of three), but also for relational experiences in elementary school and beyond. How are these two findings consistent with a left-dominant strategy? Nonverbal signals and autobiographical memory are also dominant on the right side of the brain! Shutting off the use of this side of the brain in these attachment settings would allow a person to avoid the distress from not having those needs for connection and attunement met in the past. The problem is that this adaptive strategy leaves the individual continuing to create disconnection emotionally in the present. Even the narrative descriptions of how they understand life "dismiss" the importance of being close in relationships—and in this way their strategy is called "dismissing."

We see this pattern of a focus on the outside, physical world and not on the inner world of the mind all the time with the adolescents and adults we work with in our respective practices. They look at the world as if all that really exists is its physical aspect—that which is touchable, measurable, weighable—and they see reality as existing solely on this externally visible plane of existence. And of course the physical world is real. But equally real is the inner mental and emotional side, the subjective internal sea that fills us with feelings and thoughts, hopes and dreams, impulses and desires and longings. While these are called subjective, that doesn't make them unreal; it just makes them something that begins within us. They may not be measurable, but they are arguably one of the most, if not the most, important aspects of creating well-being in our inner and interpersonal lives.

When kids are avoidantly attached to a particular caregiver, that attachment figure displays an astonishing blindness to the sea inside them: Children haven't experienced their caregivers seeing and responding to their inner world. It's as if their inner subjective selves were rarely if ever seen, acknowledged, or spoken about in what are called "reflective dialogues," or conversations about the inner nature of the mind. (More on that soon.) But the outcome of this type of attachment relationship is that it seems to create within these children a blockage that prevents them from knowing their own inner world as well. Mindsight is in short supply. The ability to see the sea inside is there, it just hasn't been developed—yet. (And again, this is true for both the parent and the child—it's never too late to develop this innate mindsight capacity.)

That's why these children understandably grow into adults with a certain "state of mind with respect to attachment," the term for how an adult carries their strategy of adapting to their own attachment history forward into their relational lives. In this case, the kind of strategy seems dominated by a way of being oblivious to the sea inside—both of oneself and of others. Attachment science reveals that avoidantly attached children tend to develop what's called *dismissing attachment* as adults. They come to live emotionally distant lives, dismissive of the importance of relationships, often avoiding closeness and rejecting attempts to relate on a deep or meaningful level. They might become immensely successful in certain areas of their lives—possibly even developing excellent social skills in a public setting—but because of their discomfort with intimacy, they essentially dismiss the importance of close relationships and thus live without that deeper connection personally. Externally they may act as if their reward drive for closeness is not present and their mindsight networks are not engaged—but these may each be a strategy to keep their bodily regulation functioning. Becoming a "we" didn't happen in a reliable way as a child, so living as a solo self may be the useful adaptation to that lack of connection earlier in life. As a result, their partners may often experience loneliness and emotional distance, and their own children are primed to develop the exact same way of relating with the world. The parental approach of an adult with a dismissing attachment pattern, then, is vastly different from that of a parent with a secure, free pattern.

Think about the classic "boo-who" knock-knock joke. The punch line perfectly communicates a dismissing parenting pattern.

Parent: Knock knock.
Child: Who's there?
Parent: Boo.
Child: Boo who?
Parent: Quit crying.

This dismissing response results from the parents' experience of never having their own emotional needs perceived and met. In stark contrast, when parents respond with attunement and caring, the response looks very different.

Parent: Knock knock.
Child: Who's there?
Parent: Boo.
Child: Boo who?
Parent: Awww, are you crying? Come in. Tell me about it.

The wordplay in the latter joke may not work as well, but the communication of love and attention certainly does.

Child Attachment Pattern	Parenting Tendencies	Child's Wired Assumptions
Secure	*Secure* attachment pattern: Sensitive, attuned, responsive to baby's bid for connection; an ability to read child's cues and predictably meet child's needs. Parent reliably "shows up" for child.	My parent isn't perfect, but I know I am safe. If I have a need she will see it and respond quickly and sensitively. I can trust that other people will do that, too. My inner experience is real and worthy of being expressed and respected.
Insecure: Avoidant	*Dismissing* attachment pattern: Indifference to child's signals and needs; lack of attunement to child's emotional needs.	My parent may be around a lot, but he doesn't care about what I need or how I feel, so I'll learn to ignore my own emotions and avoid communicating my needs.
Insecure: Ambivalent		
Insecure: Disorganized		

Ambivalent and Preoccupied Attachment

The second of the three insecure patterns, ambivalent attachment, results in adults who have a different set of challenges in relating to their own children. Kids with the avoidant attachment we just discussed typically grow up to be disconnected adults—disconnected from others and from their own inner world—who avoid emotion because of their dismissing pattern of attachment. It's simply the way they've learned to survive. This survival strategy may minimize attachment in part by being a neurological retreat to the logical, linguistic left hemisphere of the brain.

In stark contrast, *ambivalently attached* children become adults who live with a great deal of chaos, anxiety, and insecurity. Instead of living in an emotional desert, their responses to life typically involve an emotional flood. Their tumultuous experience results from having parents who sometimes showed up for them, and sometimes didn't. This "intermittent reinforcement"—this inconsistency in how their parents showed up for them—actually can be seen to increase their need for attachment. They learned that they couldn't count on their parents for attunement, connection, and regulation, and this inconsistency left them full of insecurity about the relationship with the parent and the world at large. As a result they adapted by becoming adults without a clear sense of inner security regarding close relationships. Unlike the avoidantly attached child who minimizes the drive for connection, the ambivalently attached child magnifies that drive.

Let's go back to the hungry four-month-old and look at her through this ambivalent attachment lens. When she cries, her father might actually *want* to show up for her and meet her needs. In fact, he does so at times. But sometimes his emotions overwhelm him and he becomes literally incapable of responding effectively to his daughter. Whereas the dismissing father above approached his daughter in an emotionally disconnected way, this father becomes easily flooded with emotions, leaving him muddled and confused, unable to tune in to his child and take appropriate action. Rather than addressing his daughter's hunger, he becomes anxious and worries that he won't be able to soothe her. He runs to her and, with a distressed look, picks her up. The stress he's feeling reminds him of the stress at work and his boss's criticism, which makes him think of the way his own mother used to insult him at times. Since he himself has an anxious, ambivalent history, he doubts his capacity as a father. If dismissing attachment is about disconnection, the preoccupied adult attachment is about confusion. He wants to care for his young daughter, but he's terrified that he won't be able to do it right. You may be able to imagine how in this situation, the three attachment-based networks of reward, body regulation, and mindsight all come out of balance. In this father's brain, his ambivalent attachment history enhances the reward circuitry activation, makes his body more distressed, and his mindsight lens clouded by his past unworked through issues of his own childhood experiences. All of this occurs while the baby cries in his arms, looking up at his worried face and feeling the tension in his body. She soaks in his internal state, and since he's feeling anxious and confused, she experiences it as well, picking up on his "leftover" issues of continuing insecurity.

The baby, through this and hundreds of other interactions as she grows up, learns that she can't count on her needs being perceived or met with any certainty. Her father *wants* to show up for her, and he does so at times. But more often than not, he is so consistently drowning in his own emotional world that he's unable to provide the dependable and stable presence she needs from him. As she grows into adolescence and adulthood, then, her sense of self can become very confused. Reward, body regulation, and mindsight for her, too, are not on stable footing. All she knows as a four-month-old is that she's hungry. But as she grows up, that hunger becomes neurologically connected to anxiety and uncertainty because of similar repeated ex-

Inconsistent attunement leads to insecure ambivalent attachment.

periences she has with her father and his inconsistent presence in her life. As a result, her own approach to life can become unstable and chaotic. (This is assuming she doesn't have another important caregiver who provides secure attachment that mitigates the negative effects of her ambivalent relationship with her father.)

Kids with this ambivalent attachment pattern develop what's called, in adults, a *preoccupied* attachment pattern, which is characterized by this chaotic and highly emotional way of connecting in close relationships. Whereas adults with a dismissing attachment pattern generally write off the importance of the past, along with their own and others' emotions, adults with a preoccupied attachment pattern are just the opposite. They become obsessed, or preoccupied, with the past and fixated on relationships and emotions. Their relational lives are thus characterized by high-emotion turmoil and significant anxiety. They may often have difficulty managing their needs with the people they care about, and they consistently give rein to their big emotions, like anger, resentment, and fear of past relationships. It creates within them a conflict in that their volcano of emotions can sometimes produce a fundamental passivity in their responses to the world, as feelings of shame and self-doubt leave them with that confused core self. They experience an urgency for connection that pushes others away, thus creating a feedback loop that reinforces their impression that others are not dependable. Their magnified attachment drive is filled with worry and confusion. Trust issues then predictably arise, and the cycle continues, reinforcing the very internal states that may have contributed to the confusion.

Brain scans bear this out. Researchers have looked at neuronal responses of various subjects when they are exposed to the faces and emotions of others. Whereas people with dismissing attachment spend fewer attentional resources on faces and emotions, leaving them less capable of understanding and empathizing with others, those with a preoccupied attachment are just the opposite. Their scans show that they give faces and emotions way *too much* attention, which produces a neediness that is often perceived by others. Securely attached people, as you would expect, find a healthy balance between the two responses, giving an appropriate amount of attention to relationships and the opinions of others.

The preoccupied knock-knock joke would emphasize the parent's inability to show up for her child because of her own emotional instability:

Parent: Knock knock.
Child: Who's there?
Parent: Boo.
Child: Boo who?
Parent: Are you serious? You're crying? Why are you sad? Oh, that's just great. Now you're making me cry!

Child Attachment Pattern	Parenting Tendencies	Child's Wired Assumptions
Secure	*Secure* attachment pattern: Sensitive, attuned, responsive to baby's bid for connection; an ability to read child's cues and predictably meet child's needs. Parent reliably "shows up" for child.	My parent isn't perfect, but I know I am safe. If I have a need she will see it and respond quickly and sensitively. I can trust that other people will do that, too. My inner experience is real and worthy of being expressed and respected.
Insecure: Avoidant	*Dismissing* attachment pattern: Indifference to child's signals and needs; lack of attunement to child's emotional needs.	My parent may be around a lot, but he doesn't care about what I need or how I feel, so I'll learn to ignore my own emotions and avoid communicating my needs.
Insecure: Ambivalent	*Preoccupied* attachment pattern: Sometimes attuned, sensitive, and responsive to child's signals and needs, and sometimes not. Sometimes intrusive.	I never know how my parent will respond, so I have to stay constantly on edge. I can't ever let my guard down. I can't trust that people will predictably be there for me.
Insecure: Disorganized		

Looking at this chart as we fill it in, you can see the distinctions among the various attachment patterns, and why secure, free attachment leads to such security and success in relationships and life. That freedom affords individuals the autonomy to reflect on and learn from the past, as well as from their emotions and those of others. There's no need to disconnect from them (as those with a dismissing pattern do) or to become entangled with them (as in the case of a preoccupied pattern).

Disorganized and Unresolved Attachment

The final type of insecure attachment, *disorganized attachment,* is the most troubling of all in terms of the child's development. It occurs when a parent, instead of helping the child feel safe from a threat, actually becomes the threat. The child experiences the parent as a source of terror because of repeated experiences where the parent's behavior is extremely neglectful and therefore terrifying, or excessively chaotic and overwhelming, or when the parent becomes threatening, dangerous, or frightening. Each of these conditions evokes a state of terror in the child due to the actions—or lack thereof—of the attachment figure, the parent. This experience of feeling afraid of her parent leads the child to grow into an adult who has difficulty regulating her emotions and feeling safe in the world. The other types of insecure attachment interactions, the avoidant and the ambivalent, lead to *organized* patterns of behavior that allow them to navigate their world: Dismissing individuals avoid emotional connection and intimacy due to their avoidant history with their parent; preoccupied individuals tend to experience repeating states of confusion and distress, trying the best they can to reduce the anxiety and ambivalence they feel in relationships. The key point is that minimizing attachment in avoidant/dismissing patterns, or maximizing attachment with ambivalent/preoccupied patterns, is compatible with an organized strategy to survive that's internally cohesive, if not secure or optimal.

But for adults who as children had parents who were terrifying and now have a disorganized attachment pattern, there is no such organizing strategy to navigate the world. They're left in a situation to which there is no rational or effective response. Imagine the three networks of reward, body regulation, and mindsight. With the terror of disorganized attachment, the body's dysregulation in that threat state is coupled with seeing the mind of the terrifying parent as itself terrifying. The reward basis of attachment may likely then become fragmented. Why? When a parent becomes the source of terror in a child, it creates within the child what can be called a biological paradox, as she enters into two simultaneous brain states. On one hand, she feels compelled to turn to her caregiver to help her because she is afraid. Centuries of evolutionary development have taught her brain that this is the appropriate response. Her attachment figure is supposed to protect her, to want good things for her, to provide safety and security. On the other hand, though, her caregiver in this instance is the *source* of her distress. All of those expectations she's been engineered to work from are being violated. As a result, she feels compelled to both turn to and flee from her parent.

To put it neurologically, the deep brain stem survival reactions to flee from danger drive the child to move away from the source of terror. The limbic areas, a bit higher in the downstairs brain from the brain stem, are where a majority of the attachment systems functions arise. That mammalian system basically says, "Hey! I am in danger here, all of my mammalian ancestors found comfort and safety with their attachment figures, so I am heading toward one right now!" But the attachment figure is also the source of terror. The brain stem's drive to move *away from* that figure and the limbic area's drive to move *toward* that figure result in an internal conflict, a paradox. How can one body move both toward and away from the same individual? No can do. So organized ways of dealing with this situation are simply not possible.

The ensuing fragmentation of the individual's coping strategies, what are called dissociation and severe emotional and behavioral dysregulation, create the most intense compromises to healthy functioning. Relationships are challenging, as is staying focused under stress and keeping an internal calmness in the face of a challenging inner and interpersonal life.

Attachment researcher Peter Fonagy uses a term called "epistemic trust" to study how the way we come to know the nature of reality—

epistemology—is violated especially with disorganized attachment experiences. When terrifying events are caused by the attachment figure, the nature of what is real is shaped in such a manner as to be inconsistent with the larger world of how parents are supposed to behave. Repeated violations of this epistemic trust can fragment an internal sense of what is real, and this violation may play a role in the fragmented mental life, the dissociation, that is found with individuals with disorganized attachment histories. Fortunately with intervention, such terrifying and fragmenting experiences and the dissociation they induce in a child that persist into adulthood are quite amenable to treatment and healing. But left on their own, such disorganized attachment reactions can be a part of how the next generation may again experience the terror of parents whose minds fragment and whose behaviors are again terrifying for their offspring, even if they do not in any way intend for this history to be repeated.

Parents with signs of disorganized and disoriented attachment often zigzag back and forth between chaos and rigidity, encountering severe problems when it comes to relating to others and regulating their actions and emotions. For these adults, all bets are off when threat or loss comes up. Their response can be completely disorganized and even at times dangerous. They might suddenly become enraged or threatening, lashing out verbally or physically. They might become lost in fear. Or they might even shut down, dissociating to the extent that they shift their sense of identity or lose track of what's going on. These unpredictable and frightening responses typify what's called an *unresolved* attachment pattern that we see in some adults.

For example, the father with the hungry four-month-old, if he is working from an unresolved attachment pattern, may become unable to regulate himself when he hears his baby crying. Just imagine how his reward, body regulation, and mindsight networks do not work in an organized manner given his unresolved attachment state. What might be simply a trying situation for most parents becomes almost traumatic for him—evoking in his brain states of neural acti-

vation that resemble times when tears led to terror in his own childhood. He might hurry to his daughter and pick her up abruptly in a
tense state, holding her too tightly, causing her to cry, which makes
him hold her even tighter. He might go to the kitchen to prepare her
bottle, but faced with the tension-filled situation, he feels helpless
and his mind begins to fragment. As the cries become louder, panic
washes over him, and memories of being mistreated by his own alcoholic father flood him and cause his heart to beat faster and faster. He
gets lost in a memory of his father grabbing him by the hair. He soon
realizes that he has begun yelling at his daughter—"Quiet! Quiet! I
can't take it any more!"—and she has stopped crying. She is now simply staring into space, whimpering. They are both shaken, and she is
vacant.

That vacancy is the child's response to the terror she experiences
while witnessing her father's actions. He is both frightened and
frightening, producing the biological paradox where she's driven to
flee both from and to her caregiver. This situation is obviously problematic and confusing to the child's mind, which can become fragmented. There's no way she can make sense of the situation or develop
an organized adaptation. With the other types of insecure attachment, the organized forms, there are strategic, adaptive responses to
the parents' less-than-optimal behaviors. The child of a dismissing
parent quickly learns to ignore his feelings and avoid causing trouble
or communicating needs and emotions. Likewise, the child of a preoccupied parent figures out how important it is to remain hypervigilant, ready to adapt to an unpredictable caregiver. The tenacity of
these adaptations can be seen in how deeply the child re-creates these
types of relationships in the future based on the patterns he learns to
adapt to in his response to the parent's actions.

But here, when the disorganized, unresolved actions of the parent
rear up in terrifying ways, the child is unable to devise an adaptive
response that makes any sense. There's no organized strategy or coping mechanism, since the parent's behavior is terrifying and without
organization or order. It's simply fright without a solution. The result

Terror leads to insecure, disorganized attachment.

is a fragmentation of the usual continuity of consciousness, giving rise to the experience of a dissociative mind that is challenged in regulating emotion, dealing with other people, handling frustration, and simply moving through life at times in a coherent manner.

That's why this attachment pattern is called "disorganized." One situation where this attachment pattern arises is with trauma. Scans have shown that parental abuse and neglect—what are called developmental trauma—compromise areas of the brain that enable neural integration, which may explain problems with regulation of emotion, deficient social communication, poor academic reasoning, a tendency toward interpersonal violence, and other problems seen in kids with disorganized attachment.

It probably won't come as a surprise, then, that many parents who (often unintentionally) engage in terrifying behaviors—even not considered abuse or neglect—that lead to disorganized attachment have typically themselves experienced all sorts of trauma and loss that remain unresolved. The parents' interactions with their own children are intricately interwoven with their experiences with their own caregivers.

Let's say, for example, that a child is asserting himself, not wanting to have his mother put him in his car seat. Imagine that the mother grew up with a disorganized attachment pattern as a result of the abuse she received from her father, who favored her siblings and never abused them as he did her. Her childhood experiences can greatly impact her response to her son's refusal to let her buckle him up. When he says, "You're not going to put me in my seat. Only Daddy can!" she might remain calm at first and say, "No, I'm going to do it this time."

But when the child insists, "No, Daddy!" a memory embedded in her nervous system—an experience woven into the narrative of who she is—intrudes on her mind and quickly takes over. She recalls the feeling of abandonment when her father favored her siblings, along with the terror when he, the one who was supposed to protect her, went after her to beat her. The betrayal, the humiliation, the abandonment, the panic: It all became embedded in what's called her "implicit memory," in her emotional, perceptual, bodily memory. And in this moment, it primes the brain to spring into action.

So when her two-year-old says, "Daddy's going to buckle me in, not you!" this mother's brain, still full of unresolved trauma, gives way to those implicit memories. She simply reacts, unaware that what she's doing is related to her unresolved past experiences. She feels humiliated by her son. Desperate to be a competent mother, she insists, "Get in your car seat!" But she's again told, "No, no, no. You don't know how to do it right!" Then that sense of incompetence as a parent resonates with the humiliation from her own childhood. Shame, abandonment, betrayal, and all kinds of other emotions swirl within her, and she grabs her small son and tries to force him into the car seat.

In ten seconds, from the time they reached the car until this moment, she has lost control. All of that implicit, subcortical memory has become activated, and the lower, primitive, downstairs part of her brain has taken over. Who knows where it goes from there? In an extreme case she might eventually collapse in hopelessness, run back inside, or fall to the floor crying and screaming as she is lost in an implicit memory. She might feel completely afraid of who she's become in that moment. Just as likely, she'll get angry and become not only verbally and emotionally abusive, but even physically hurtful as well.

This is what can result from disorganized attachment, and we can see how these incidents of terrifying parental dysregulation, while unintended, can emerge from its counterpart, unresolved adult attachment. The confusing, disorganized cycle of parent-child interactions repeats itself, creating individuals unable to cope when life's challenges appear. They have no clear sense of who they are or how to engage in healthy relationships. The disorganized knock-knock joke would be completely nonsensical, leaving the child utterly lost as to how to respond to his mother's chaos and disorientation:

Parent: Knock knock.
Child: Who's there?
Parent: Boo.
Child: Boo who?
Parent: Boo who yourself! I hate you, you crybaby. Get out of
    my room!

Child Attachment Pattern	Parenting Tendencies	Child's Wired Assumptions
Secure	*Secure* attachment pattern: Sensitive, attuned, responsive to baby's bid for connection; an ability to read child's cues and predictably meet child's needs. Parent reliably "shows up" for child.	My parent isn't perfect, but I know I am safe. If I have a need she will see it and respond quickly and sensitively. I can trust that other people will do that, too. My inner experience is real and worthy of being expressed and respected.
Insecure: Avoidant	*Dismissing* attachment pattern: Indifference to child's signals and needs; lack of attunement to child's emotional needs.	My parent may be around a lot, but he doesn't care about what I need or how I feel, so I'll learn to ignore my own emotions and avoid communicating my needs.
Insecure: Ambivalent	*Preoccupied* attachment pattern: Sometimes attuned, sensitive, and responsive to child's signals and needs, and sometimes not. Sometimes intrusive.	I never know how my parent will respond, so I have to stay constantly on edge. I can't ever let my guard down. I can't trust that people will predictably be there for me.
Insecure: Disorganized	*Unresolved* attachment pattern: At times severely unattuned to child's signals and needs; disorienting; either frightening, frightened, or both.	My parent is terrifying and disorienting. I'm not safe, and there is no one to keep me safe. I don't know what to do. I am helpless. People are scary and unreliable.

Now that the chart is completely filled in, you can see why the disorganized attachment pattern is so dysfunctional for children, as well as to the adults they become. If the extreme cases of developmental trauma of abuse and neglect are generalizable, we can see how disorganized attachment may involve significant compromises to the integration within the child's brain. When conditions similar to the initial trauma or neglect arise, this context-dependent brain state can be especially prone to activating a threat state, and the individual now in this survival mode of fragmentation can no longer be present for interaction with others, including the child.

Whereas the other forms of insecure attachment certainly cause challenges in close relationships, they at least leave kids with an organized, adaptive strategy, whether it's to shut down and disconnect from emotions (as in the case of avoidant attachment) or to amp up and remain on edge in close relationships (as in ambivalent attachment). Those at least enable children to develop consistent responses to their parents' lack of providing secure attachment: shut down or rev up. The unresolved, disorganized attachment pattern, in contrast, leaves kids confused and without any coping strategy that makes sense on any level. In some ways, disorganized attachment may be understood as involving both a revving up and a shutting down of the attachment drive as the child attempts to carry out the accompanying approach and avoid behaviors toward the same caregiver. In addition, the violation in epistemic trust—of knowing how to know what is real or not—may fill such internal disorganization with a sense of further terror and confusion. This outward behavioral paradox reinforces a dissociative internal mechanism of dealing with stress as the child matures into adolescence and beyond.

A Reason for Hope: Earned Secure Attachment

What do these often-repeated studies by attachment researchers show us? Well, again, it's pretty consistent with what we'd expect: Sensitive, attuned parents who are emotionally responsive typically raise kids who are resilient and emotionally healthy, and who generally grow up to be well-adjusted and happy adults capable of cultivating mutually rewarding relationships.

As early as a child's first birthday, it's extremely clear how much their parents influence their development and perspective on the world—both in childhood and as they become adults.

To be sure, genetics strongly influence how a child turns out, as does chance. But even as early as a child's first birthday, it's extremely clear how much their parents influence their development and perspective on the world—both in childhood and as they become adults.

Do any of these attachment patterns strike a chord with you? Do you recognize your own parents—or maybe yourself—in any of these descriptions? If some of the insecure or unresolved patterns resonate with you, we have a message of great hope: Even if you didn't receive secure attachment from your parents, you can still offer it to your own children. Secure attachment can be *learned and earned.*

We know we want to be sensitive and attuned to our children, and to help them grow up with a secure attachment. So what do we do if we find ourselves exhibiting some of the characteristics of an avoidant, or ambivalent, or disorganized attachment? Are we doomed to repeat the same patterns?

"Absolutely not" is the extremely encouraging message that attachment science offers. People often believe that early attachment experiences are important and immutable. And while they are very important, they are absolutely changeable. This is where *earned secure attachment* comes in. You can earn security by learning how to be in secure relationships. Yes, the way you were parented significantly influences the way you view the world and parent your children. But what's even more crucial is how you've made sense of your own childhood experiences—how your mind shapes your memories to explain who you are in the present. While you can't change the past, you can change how you come to make sense of it. If you can look at your own life story, especially at your parents, and understand why they behaved as they did, you can gain an awareness of how your childhood experiences impacted your development and continue to affect your current relationships, including the way you parent your own children. This is how you learn to earn secure attachment. In the coming pages we'll discuss how your interactions with your children can be a key element in the process of making sense of your own attachment history.

What does it mean, specifically, to make sense of our life story? As we've said, the key is to develop what attachment scientists call a "coherent narrative," where we reflect on and acknowledge both positive and negative aspects of our family experiences and how we feel about them. Then we can learn how these experiences impacted our brains and our models for relationships. For example, a section of a coherent narrative might sound something like this: "My mother was always angry. She loved us; there was never any doubt about that. But her parents had really done a number on her. Her dad worked all the time, and her mom was a closet alcoholic. Mom was the oldest of six kids, so she always felt like she had to be perfect. But obviously, she couldn't. She bottled everything up and tried to stay in ultimate control, but her emotions just boiled over anytime something went wrong. My sisters and I usually took the brunt of it, sometimes even physically. I worry that sometimes I let my kids get away with too much, and I think part of that is because I don't want them to feel that pressure to be perfect."

Like many of us, this woman obviously had a childhood that was less than ideal. But she can talk clearly about it, even finding compassion for her mother, and reflect on what it all means for herself and her children. She can offer specific details about her experience, moving easily from memory to understanding. She's not dismissing the past or becoming preoccupied with it. That's a coherent narrative.

Many people who are securely attached as adults grew up with parents who, while not perfect, did a good job most of the time consistently responding to their children's needs. But other people are like this woman and must "earn" their secure attachment, meaning that even though their parents didn't present them with the kind of childhood that would lead to secure attachment as adults, they overcame this obstacle by making sense of what they went through. That making-sense process can happen via internal reflections or inter-personal connections.

In contrast, adults who haven't earned secure attachment by doing this emotional work have difficulty telling their life story in a lucid and intelligible way. With a dismissing pattern, for instance, a person's narrative will often be disjointed and reflect a rejection of the importance of relationships, emotions, and the past. No matter how articulate such individuals may be, when it comes to reflecting on their family and early life experiences, they may find it difficult to tell a coherent story that makes sense of their childhood experiences. When asked about their early family life, they may not be willing or able to recall specific memories from childhood, particularly the emotional and relational details of experiences. They might insist that their mother was "loving" but remain unable to give any specific memories to support that statement. Their stories from childhood may reflect isolation and growing up in an emotionally and relationally barren environment, and they might insist, "It's fine, though. I don't like all that drama anyway." As we mentioned, this lack of access to autobiographical memory and reflection may in part be connected to a neurological adaptation: avoidance born of the decreased development of the right hemisphere's autobiographical memory and sense of the body's signals.

Or, in contrast, the person might pay so much attention to the details of their past that they actually become lost in them. This would be evidence of a preoccupied attachment pattern, where the person offers a confusing narrative that blends past events with recent occurrences from their adult life. The preoccupied pattern gets its name because the narrative becomes preoccupied with relationships, emotions, and the past. We may view this as excessive flooding of right-hemisphere autobiographical memory and the emotionally activated states arising from the body. The person with a preoccupied pattern has a hard time staying on topic, and easily gets flooded in the recollection, leaving the story disconnected and confusing.

In the final insecure pattern, unresolved attachment, a person may have experienced the fright-without-solution described earlier, where parents were terrified and/or terrifying. As you might now anticipate, this type of relational trauma as a child also often results in narratives that interfere with clear and lucid communication about the past once the child grows up. In this case, an unresolved attachment pattern leads the person's narrative to become incoherent, particularly when asked about the topics of threat, fear, death, or anything related to the person's trauma. They may get lost in details and even, as they tell their story, experience an altered consciousness like dissociation or a trance-like state, resulting in a story that is fundamentally fragmented.

Whether people are working from a dismissing, preoccupied, or unresolved attachment pattern, they are unable to tell a coherent story about their past—each in their own unique pattern of incoherence. And without a coherent narrative, they will have difficulty understanding where they've been and how they've become the people that they are. In the case of parents, they'll be likely to repeat the mistakes of their own caregivers as they raise their children; they'll pass down the relational-pattern legacy they inherited that wired their brains in less-than-optimal ways.

However, when we gather the courage to examine our past, and develop the ability to reflect on and then tell our own stories in a clear and coherent way—where we are neither running from the past nor becoming preoccupied with it—we can begin to heal from our past wounds. In doing so, we rewire our brains so we can better enable our children to form a secure attachment with us, and that solid relationship will become a source of resilience throughout their lives.

It can be an incredibly liberating experience to realize that you're not to blame for your parents' failure to show up for you in your childhood, and that you have the power to liberate yourself now from a past you did not create.

Then, out of that liberation, you can begin taking responsibility for your behavior going forward, what we clinicians call *agency*. As one parent put it, "I'm not to blame for what happened to me. But I *am* responsible for what I do now." The truth is that we've become the people we are and developed the behavioral patterns we have because

they were a part of strategies enabling us to adapt to our particular situations. We find strategies to survive and do as best we can. In other words, along the way we adapted to our circumstances, and we did what we needed to survive in our families, especially as children. But as adults, those patterns of survival strategies may have become a prison. And those very strategies may have deeply affected our reward systems' drive for attachment, the ways we sense and regulate our body's state, and the way we come to have mindsight and know the internal mental life of ourselves and others.

When we gather the courage to examine our past, and develop the ability to reflect on and then tell our own stories in a clear and coherent way—where we are neither running from the past nor becoming preoccupied with it—we can begin to heal from our past wounds. In doing so, we rewire our brains so we can better enable our children to form a secure attachment with us, and that solid relationship will become a source of resilience throughout their lives.

But we don't have to stay stuck there; you can become liberated from the confinement created by your experiences. Just as relationships can and do change, attachment patterns can and do change as well. When we come to "make sense" of our lives, it's not simply an intellectual exercise. It actually reorganizes our sense of reward, body regulation, and insight. Making sense is a deeply integrative process at the core of who we are and how we become a part of a "we" in close relationships. And for our parenting, making sense of our own lives, research shows, can liberate us to become the parents we want to be.

Children who experience a transformation in how their caregiver connects with them can undergo a change in their own attachment pattern. The same is true for adults. Being with a life partner who is securely attached as an adult can help someone with insecurity move toward a more free, connected pattern of relating to others. We are always open to change! Security can be earned, and it can be learned. Dan once worked with someone in his nineties who transformed his relational strategies, his adult attachment pattern, toward a more freely loving way he could show up for his spouse and his whole family. His wife even asked Dan if he had given her husband a "brain transplant."

We don't have to let our past experiences dominate the way we live our lives and parent our own children. We can change the narrative, and thereby alter the future for our kids and grandkids.

In short, we don't have to let our past experiences dominate the way we live our lives and parent our own children. We can change the narrative, and thereby alter the future for our kids and grandkids.

In fact, research shows that even when parents have to earn their security later in life by creating a coherent narrative, they can parent their kids as effectively as those who had more optimal childhoods and were fortunate enough to receive what's called "continual secure attachment."

For years Dan has used a helpful analogy for confronting our past. If trauma is like a dog bite, we can understand how our natural impulse is to pull away from it. So if a dog bites you on the hand, and you pull your hand away, he digs his teeth in even more strongly and your struggle worsens the injury of the bite. But if instead you shove your hand down the dog's throat, he'll gag and actually release his grip on your hand, minimizing the damage and optimizing the healing. Trauma is just like that. We naturally pull away from reflecting on the trauma, not wanting to be flooded by the painful memories or thinking, "It's the past, so what's the point of dwelling on something you can't change?" But in reality, memory retrieval when combined with narrative reflections can be a memory modifier. Unresolved loss or trauma can be healed, and the coherent narrative that emerges can help us to be all the stronger because of that very process of making sense of your life. Some call that "post-traumatic growth." No one is asking you to create loss, abuse, or neglect; but if they do occur, harnessing your courage and the power of your mind and your close relationships to aim your attention straight at that loss and trauma will be a gift you offer yourself. "Let everything be a teacher in life" is a strong strategy of how we can learn to thrive in the face of the inevitable and unexpected challenges life throws our way. Challenges can be viewed as opportunities for growth. You'll heal the wounds, and strengthen your presence and love, from your inner strength and from the relational world of now-rewarding connections with others.

For some this can be a relatively simple process of reflecting on your past and learning to narrate an understanding of, say, your father and his dismissing attachment pattern. For example, you might look at his history and understand that he grew up in poverty with parents who worked such long hours that they were unable to show up for him, emotionally. Maybe they responded, any time he was upset, by saying, "Stop whining. You should count your blessings." As a result, he may have been left with an avoidant attachment pattern that led to his dismissing parenting approach with his own children. He may have been largely left-brain dominant in relating to others, missing their nonverbal signals and having a limited autobiographical sense of self to share with those close to him, or himself. This new awareness can lead you to feel compassion for your father, where you can say, "He really let me down as a father, but I can see why. He was never given the emotional skills or resources by his own parents. No wonder he didn't know how to show up for me in deeper and more meaningful ways. That was painful for me and I felt alone a lot, and I want to make sure I have a close, connected relationship with my kids where they know they can come to me. I want to sense their minds, even if that wasn't a part of my childhood back then."

For others, the process can be much more complex and even at times painful. It might serve you well to get some help along the way. Psychotherapy, for example, often becomes a powerful tool to help us make sense of our stories. The therapy relationship, in fact, can simulate a secure attachment relationship, giving you the experience of feeling safe, seen, soothed, and secure as you begin to understand and pull together the threads of your parents' stories, even helping you empathize with their experiences, and why they failed to be the kind of parents you needed. Most important, therapy can help integrate your brain, as it integrates the past and present to allow you to communicate and be present with your child in ways that build secure attachment now and in the future.

We all need to develop a coherent narrative, where we can "tell the story" of our childhood—usually not to our kids, but to ourselves or those adults close to us. Reflecting on our experiences with our parents and other caregivers who impacted our development is important, and equally crucial is how we had to deal with what we experienced, or what we missed.

Without a coherent narrative, we're likely to repeat the mistakes our parents made, passing down the painful legacy they learned from their own caregivers. But when we make sense of our experiences and work to comprehend our parents' own woundedness, we can break the cycle and avoid passing down the inheritance of insecure attachment.

Remember, we all are born with a drive for connection, even if we never got to enjoy loving relationships as children. And so we feel the lack of close connection, though often beneath awareness, and we need to understand that pain of what's missing in our life. Because without this coherent narrative, we're likely to repeat the mistakes our parents made, passing down the painful legacy they learned from their own caregivers.

But when we make sense of our experiences and work to comprehend our parents' own woundedness, we can break the cycle and avoid passing down the inheritance of insecure attachment. You may wonder about forgiveness. A colleague and friend, Jack Kornfield, has a great way of thinking about this important process: Forgiveness is giving up all hope for a better past. In this way, we forgive not to condone, not to say it was fine, but to let go of false illusions that we can change the past. The acceptance and forgiveness that arise with making sense of your life are profoundly liberating. In many ways, we come to forgive ourselves for the adaptations we had to make, and to accept not only who we've been, but who we are now inviting ourselves to become.

> By doing your own personal inner work and earning a secure attachment, you break the cycle of insecure attachment and improve the lives of generations who follow you.

It's rarely easy, but just think about what a gift you're giving your kids when you do this important work of understanding the story of your own childhood, both the joys and the pain. When you develop this coherent narrative about your past, you can become the parent you want to be, and you can pass down to your children a secure attachment that allows them to feel connected to you in strong and meaningful ways. Then, guess who else receives that gift? That's right, your grandchildren. And great-grandchildren. By doing your own personal inner work and earning a secure attachment, you break the cycle of insecure attachment and improve the lives of generations who follow you.

So that's our primary, heartfelt message to you as we explore in the coming chapters what it means, specifically, to show up for your kids: Regardless of your upbringing, and whatever happened to you in your past, you can be the loving, sensitive parent you want to be, the one who shows up and raises kids who are happy, successful, and fully themselves.

Regardless of your upbringing, and whatever happened to you in your past, you can be the loving, sensitive parent you want to be, the one who shows up and raises kids who are happy, successful, and fully themselves.

Beginning with the next chapter, we're going to get very specific about how you can cultivate just that kind of relationship with your kids. Along the way, we'll give you further opportunities to consider your own attachment history, and how it affects your interactions with your children.

$\underline{S}$afe

CHAPTER 3

Beyond Helmets and Kneepads
Helping Your Child Feel SAFE

n the previous chapter we focused on the importance of taking the time to more fully understand your own history and how it impacts the way you interact with your children. Now let's return to the Four S's—making kids feel safe, seen, soothed, and secure—and go deeper into what it means to really show up for our kids. The very first thing we have to do for our kids is to keep them safe. That's why safety is the first S.

It may seem obvious that a caregiver's job is to keep kids safe. But in talking to parents all over the world, we've come to learn that many caregivers—even involved, attentive parents who clearly want what's best for their kids—haven't really thought deeply about what it means to keep their children safe. Some of what we say here may surprise you. Some of it may even make you feel uncomfortable. If what we say in the coming pages doesn't touch you or seem relevant, then that's great. You may have already created the bedrock of safety in your child's life, which is the foundation for everything else we'll say in the coming chapters. But in our experience as parents and as clinicians, we know that many caregivers, maybe even most of us, have kids who at least sometimes experience fear because of something we ourselves have said or done. And as we'll soon explain, when kids are fearful or feel threatened in some way, they don't feel safe. A threat response in their bodies and brains becomes activated, and that response feels like the opposite of safety. So as you read this chapter, we ask that you keep an open mind, and see whether what we say here might be relevant for your child. The research indicates that abuse, neglect, and other adverse childhood experiences that create states of fear are far more common in children's lives than most people realize. This means that even if you feel confident in your own approach with your kids, there are likely people in your life—a partner, or a family member or caregiver—who have been or will be affected by a violation of the safety foundation we're addressing in this chapter.

Let's begin by defining our terms. When we talk about helping kids feel safe, we're talking about physical as well as emotional and relational safety. For example, let us tell you about Kaitlin, a fifth grader who seemingly has it all going for her. She's healthy and bright, she has two parents who are still married, and while the family isn't rich, they have plenty of food and a clean, reliable, and seemingly stable place to live without any apparent threats that might harm her. She's perfectly safe, in other words—at least when viewed from the outside.

Her world behind closed doors, however, is starkly different. Especially when her father, Craig, is around. He storms through her life, frequently criticizing her and flying off the handle, yelling at her even when she's done nothing wrong. Minor infractions, like leaving her sweatshirt in the living room or forgetting to put her dinner plate in the sink, regularly produce his condemnation and often his rage. Even when she accidentally begins humming to herself while he's watching the game on a Saturday afternoon, she faces his wrath, and other times she's a frightened bystander, watching her dad screaming at her younger brother. Sometimes, when he's in an especially foul mood, he'll nitpick Kaitlin's appearance, finding fault with her clothes and even her weight.

What's clear in a situation like this is that there are definitely different types of safety. While Kaitlin's basic physical needs are taken care of, safety is the last thing she experiences when it comes to the emotional care she receives from her father. She can't even relax in her own home. She's clearly not safe on an emotional level. In fact, it's not even safe for her to express her feelings. If she cries in response to her father's anger or criticism, he belittles her, yelling, "Why do you have to be so thin-skinned? You're not a baby." Or he'll blame her for her emotional response, telling her, "You're going to have to toughen up some day."

One piece of good news in this scenario is that Kaitlin does have a person in her corner: her mother, Jennifer. And while Jennifer isn't always courageous when it comes to standing up for Kaitlin when Craig demeans her, she does provide a constant source of support and encouragement for her daughter, a haven from her father's storms. As a result, despite the fear she experiences, Kaitlin is developing a certain amount of resilience in one aspect of her functioning. She's actually managing to do well overall in various aspects of her life: She loves school and her friends, and she enjoys the various activities she participates in. However, the negative, humiliating experiences with her father will likely take a toll on her overall resilience and how her nervous system gets primed to respond to stress and conflict, making her prone to a number of vulnerabilities in her responses to challenges now and in the future. The fact that she has a primary secure attachment with her mother, the person with whom she spends the most time, will to some degree counter these adverse impacts on her development. If, in contrast, Craig were her primary caregiver with these disorganizing interactions, Kaitlin's development would likely be far more severely affected.

We hear from parents everywhere who feel worried about the way their partner is parenting: "I hate the way my husband talks to our kids, and he thinks I'm coddling them," or, "My wife just doesn't really get the idea of nurturing. It's more like she's a drill sergeant." We also frequently hear a parent expressing concern about a coparent who scares their child, yelling, screaming, getting easily frustrated, and even being too rough with their child's body. You've already heard us stress how powerful it can be for a child to have *just one* caregiver who shows up for them both physically and emotionally, and we'll discuss this idea further throughout the book. Kaitlin undergoes a wide range of experiences, both good and bad, with her parents, and the various family dynamics among the three of them demonstrate a great deal about what safety can mean in a relationship.

Safety: The Opposite of Threat

To get clear on what "safety" means in terms of secure attachment, let's begin with the fundamentals. It starts with basic survival, and taking care of our children's physical needs: food, shelter, and protection. It also refers to overall health. We try to limit fast food and encourage them to eat their vegetables. We make sure they wear sunscreen and brush their teeth. And just as important, we protect them from physical and emotional harm—either from someone else or even from us as their parents.

Our kids know that keeping them safe is our job. It's an expectation coded deep within their brains. When a threat appears in a secure relationship, our children instinctually know to come find us. Their genes, along with the brain those genes helped shape, have evolved over millennia to develop a deep, abiding, and automatic conviction that their caregiver's job is to keep them safe. So when faced with a threat, the brain sends signals that the child should find Mom or Dad or another attachment figure—immediately. All of the brain's attention, all of the body's resources, go first to survival and seeking safety.

That's been the case in mammals for our long evolutionary history. A chimp in the jungle hears something alarming, or sees a predator, and its instinct is to immediately go to an attachment figure. The attachment figure protects it: grabs it and runs, or steps between the chimp and the danger and fights. Then the threat passes, or the peril turns out only to be a branch that fell, and the caregiver has signaled to the child, "I've got you. You're going to be okay. You're safe."

Safety, then, is the opposite of threat. It's also the first step toward strong attachment: A caregiver helps the child *be* safe and therefore *feel* safe.

Safety
is the first step
toward strong
attachment: A caregiver
helps the child *be* safe
and therefore *feel*
safe.

Safety is the opposite of threat.

This sense of safety emerges from the nervous system's physiological experience of safety and creates a deep state of trust, allowing for optimal development and resilience in the face of challenges. And all of that begins with a consistent message from the caregiver: *I'm here for you. I will protect you. I am the nest, the protective home you can*

Unsafe vs. Safe
A child who feels unsafe in the world

A child who feels safe in the world

count on, and when you're afraid or in danger, I'll always be here.
Count on it. I will protect you and keep you safe.

When there's peril or the possibility of peril, parents protect. The more our kids know they can count on being safe, the more secure the child-parent attachment can become. Safety is the core aspect of our attachment experience. It allows kids to feel connected and protected.

Safety is the core aspect of our attachment experience. It allows kids to feel connected and protected.

Unfortunately, not all parents provide this kind of safety. Think about the difference between a child's perspective on the world where she feels safe, as opposed to one where she doesn't.

Safety affects, in a significant manner, the way we interact with our surroundings—from the very beginning. The regulatory circuits of the brain are largely formed in the first three years of life. Then, as a child grows and the prefrontal cortex matures throughout childhood and adolescence, much depends on whether he has experienced a general sense of safety. If not, he has to remain in a heightened state of alertness and anxiety to watch for danger and try to stay safe—on his own. He must spend large amounts of resources being hypervigilant, scanning the environment, or even his caregivers' faces, for approaching threats. If, on the other hand, his caregivers have adequately protected him and kept him safe in the world, then the child knows he'll be safeguarded and assisted when he's in distress.

The implications of this general sense of safety in the world are significant. When the child feels assured of safety, as opposed to worrying that he must face threats alone and therefore remain in fear, he can focus his attention on more productive activities that build the brain's connections. He can spend more time and resources learning, fostering social skills and networks, following passions and talents, learning to problem-solve and regulate emotions, and curiously exploring the world. Whereas threat creates a brain state of reactivity

When kids feel safe, it replenishes their inner resources.

RESOURCES

When they don't, those resources are depleted.

RESOURCES

and survival, safety creates a brain state for receptive and engaged learning, as well as optimal development.

We therefore want to fill our children's "tanks" in a way that helps them grow up knowing that they are safe in the world, both physically and emotionally, and that while there are indeed dangers out there, they can overcome challenges and emerge even stronger. This is the resilience we discuss so much throughout our books. It's why the positive presence of Kaitlin's mother in her life mitigates some of the damage inflicted by her father's frequent rage and degrading comments. There are ramifications from how well we show up—or fail to show up—for our kids. When they know we're there for them, they can enjoy a sense of safety and trust that reduces their stress and creates the conditions of an internal sense of security. That's how serving up safety offers a direct pathway toward an inner sense of well-being.

Parents' Two Main Jobs in Providing Safety

It's really pretty straightforward, then. Parents have two primary jobs when it comes to keeping their kids safe and making them feel safe. The first is to protect them from harm. The second is to avoid becoming the *source* of fear and threat.

> Parents have two primary jobs when it comes to keeping their kids safe and making them feel safe. The first is to protect them from harm. The second is to avoid becoming the *source* of fear and threat.

While there are many steps we can take to help our kids feel safe, we can also do the opposite, leaving them operating from a shaky, unstable foundation. Let's look at a few ways that we may let our children down by failing to protect them.

In the most extreme cases, we fail to protect them from traumatic experiences. A trauma can be defined as an experience that threatens our physical survival, or one that disrupts our sense of meaning—how we make sense of life. In this way, for example, a parent who comes home intoxicated and is unable to function, even if he is not attacking a child, may be creating a traumatic event in that the child cannot make sense of that new and disturbing, perhaps even terrifying, parental behavior. Abuse and neglect, especially when ongoing, are the most obvious examples of threats to a child's physical integrity, and without intervention, these can lead to lifelong challenges and have a significant impact on a child's physiology, development, and perspective on attachment and relationships. In short, significant dangers faced by a child activate the threat response and the fight-flight-freeze-faint reaction—and the key issue for attachment is when the parent is the source of that fear. When these dangers are repeated, if the child isn't protected by another caregiver, the recurring experiences may lead to the disorganized attachment discussed in the previous chapter. Practically speaking, as the research demonstrates, disorganized attachment leads to various troubling outcomes, including a fragmented sense of self; difficulty regulating emotions; trouble in close relationships; dissociation or discontinuities in consciousness when faced with challenges and stressors; and problems thinking clearly under stress. This disorganized attachment resulting from extreme developmental trauma can be disabling, even in the presence of other forms of security.

Even when parents provide appropriate supervision and are reliably protecting their children, traumatizing events not caused by parents may occur. Our world unfortunately can lead to encounters with older children, adolescents, or adults who may have been in a position of trust but become abusive to our children. Being open to this possibility means being proactive and thoughtful about situations your child might encounter and watching for any kind of change in your child's behavior that may indicate something upsetting happening outside of your care. Research suggests that you, as a reliable attachment figure, can serve as an essential home base in the event that trauma unrelated to an attachment figure occurs. It's important to know that if something traumatic does occur to your child, there are professionals who can help him process the trauma and offer interventions that can support him.

To see just how impactful early trauma can be, we want to introduce you to the Adverse Childhood Experiences (ACE) study, an ongoing collaboration between the Centers for Disease Control and Kaiser Permanente. Since 1994, more than fifteen thousand adults have been interviewed about various adverse childhood experiences (ACEs). The results have been both fascinating and disheartening, as researchers were surprised to see the prevalence of significant childhood stressors, as well as the extent to which early trauma and other negative experiences correlate with well-known risk factors like smoking, alcohol abuse, obesity, and diseases that are leading causes of death. We can provide only a brief overview of the ACE study here, but we encourage you to read more if you find the information interesting and/or relevant to your life.

Researchers asked participants about ten different ACEs that are all too common as kids grow up:

- Abuse: Emotional
- Abuse: Physical
- Abuse: Sexual
- Neglect: Emotional
- Neglect: Physical
- Household dysfunction: Domestic violence
- Household dysfunction: Substance abuse
- Household dysfunction: Mental illness
- Household dysfunction: Parental separation/divorce
- Household dysfunction: Incarcerated relative

These ten items certainly do not encompass all the undesirable experiences that children face. The list does not include, for example, having a parent with a chronic illness, growing up in a violent neighborhood, witnessing violence, spending time in an unhealthy foster home, or experiencing the death of a parent or sibling, to name only a few. Still, the study results for those ten items were remarkable. In examining these factors, researchers discovered that not only were the ten ACEs common, but they were also highly interrelated. If you have one ACE, you're likely to have others. Furthermore, it's important to note that the study showed the way a cumulative ACE score can lead to lasting negative effects throughout the life span, *assuming there's no intervention.*

A person's ACE score is how many of the individual ACEs that person has experienced. A score of 0 would mean that the person reports none of the categories. If she were to report, say, physical abuse, emotional neglect, and exposure to domestic violence, she would therefore have an ACE score of 3, since she reported three of the experiences.

What's remarkable about the score is what it reveals about what the researchers have called "the cumulative biologic effects of childhood stressors." In lay terms, that refers to how a person's score correlates to the way the brain and body function. Negative impacts on social, emotional, and cognitive development can be traced to high

ACE scores, as can health risks, disability, disease, and even early mortality. Notice what this means: When children undergo multiple adverse experiences, these are not merely painful individual moments in their lives. Rather, ACEs disrupt neurodevelopment and can have lifelong effects on children's overall health, their ability to relate to others, their capacity to handle adversity, their overall quality of life, and even their expected life span. The higher the ACE score, the greater the overall set of challenges and the greater the impact on development.

Again, it's crucial to emphasize that the study examined overall impacts, and didn't take into account whether and how children who received professional care and parental support learned to overcome adverse experiences. If you'd like to read about how you can help individuals who have experienced great amounts of adversity, we recommend Nadine Burke Harris's book *The Deepest Well*. It demonstrates that it is indeed possible to overcome even significant trauma. Therefore, while we should obviously try to prevent trauma, we have every reason to feel great optimism that with intervention, these negative impacts can be ameliorated.

One major conclusion of the study is how important it is to understand more about ACEs, since doing so can help address and prevent some of the worst health and social problems society faces. Further, educators, childcare workers, healthcare providers, and other professionals need to be trauma-informed to understand the impact that trauma has on behavior, regulation, and learning, so that challenging behavior can be better understood and appropriate and helpful interventions can be put in place. Unfortunately, without a trauma-informed lens, parents, schools, organizations, and professionals may do

Educators, childcare workers, healthcare providers, and other professionals need to be trauma-informed to understand the impact that trauma has on behavior, regulation, and learning, so that challenging behavior can be better understood and appropriate and helpful interventions can be put in place.

more harm by invoking more fear through their responses to the kinds of behaviors and reactivity that often emerge as a result of trauma.

More to our point here, preventing as many ACEs as possible is what we're all about as parents. In many ways, that's what safety means. Again, the ACE study offers powerful findings, but it did not include individuals who had experienced therapeutic intervention, and it did not look at *positive* childhood experiences. So rather than feeling despair, we should feel motivated by these findings to minimize developmental adversity. Still, when ACEs do occur, we should amplify positive supportive relationships and offer interventions that can reduce their impact by lowering the stress response and improving the regulatory skills of the child.

How can we best do that? By providing secure attachment. You can see how detrimental it can be when parents don't show up with sensitive, predictable care or, worse, when they actually become the source of danger and even terror in their children. Remember, too, that only some of the various ACEs fall within the abuse category. Children can be adversely affected in all kinds of ways, including other experiences that aren't incorporated in the ACE study list.

For example, a few years ago Tina worked with a family facing a situation that is, unfortunately, more common than you might expect. The parents had divorced recently, and the mother was abusing alcohol. When her son was at her apartment and she was drinking, she was often out of control, raging and yelling at the boy and creating all kinds of fear within him. To make matters worse, when he said he was scared and asked to call his father, she wouldn't let him and became even more frightening. This kind of fear creates the biological paradox we discussed earlier, where a parent—who is supposed to offer protection from danger—becomes the source of it. This paradox, in the literature referred to as fear without resolution, can create significant emotional damage and produce a disorganized attachment pattern. As a reminder, the problem is that one interconnected set of circuits—the mammalian attachment system—is insisting that the child go *toward* the attachment figure, while another circuit—the older, reptilian threat-survival reaction system—screams, "Get away from the threat!" One body, two conflicting approach-avoid sets of commands. And there's no organized approach, so the child's mind fragments. The brain becomes disorganized and doesn't know how to process this fright-without-solution and these neurologically irreconcilable states.

Anytime parents abuse substances, they're at risk of endangering their kids, either by failing to protect them or by actively causing harm. In fact, every year, many schools have to intervene because a parent drives to the carpool circle to pick up her child and is clearly under the influence of one substance or another. If you suspect that you might be dealing with an addiction, we urge you to speak with a professional and address the issue immediately, if not for yourself, for your children. Abusing substances is one way caregivers violate the two jobs of the parent: protecting children and avoiding becoming the source of terror.

Clearly, the same goes for abuse or neglect. (Neglect, in fact, is the most common type of child trauma.) If any of this sounds familiar, or if you are aware of ways you (or someone else) is harming your child and contributing to their ACE score, we urge you to seek help. You might begin with a trusted friend, and then seek the help of a counselor, therapist, or medical doctor if necessary. You love your children, and you'd never want to have a negative impact on their development. But you likely need to get help to protect them, whether from someone else or yourself. Often, when parents abuse or neglect their children, they themselves have a history of trauma and abuse, and it's important to find the courage to

If you suspect that you might be dealing with an addiction, we urge you to speak with a professional and address the issue immediately, if not for yourself, for your children. Abusing substances is one way caregivers violate the two jobs of the parent: protecting children and avoiding becoming the source of terror.

begin healing ourselves in order to be the kind of parent who can be the source of safety instead of terror.

Dan's book with Mary Hartzell, *Parenting from the Inside Out*, would be a good guide to the steps needed to make sense of your life and free yourself up to become the parent you, deep in your heart, truly want to be. If you think about it, an upstairs brain that is fully developed has a sense of wholeness and the capacity to reflect with insight on the workings of one's own mind, as well as the empathic capacity to sense and respect what is going on inside another individual. An integrated brain state creates two key functions: insight and empathy. When abuse or neglect is present, something very wrong is going on in the parent in either what has been learned or what has become a strategy of relating to others, in which empathy and compassion are severely disengaged. Insight may also be challenged. We invite you to consider that we are all born with the capacity for love and care, and many of us have had to learn to adapt to a life with suboptimal attachment. It's never too late to reflect on what may have gone on in our own lives and then begin the repair process in our self-understanding to allow that care for ourselves to emerge.

We are all born with the capacity for love and care, and many of us have had to learn to adapt to a life with suboptimal attachment. It's never too late to reflect on what may have gone on in our own lives and then begin the repair process in our self-understanding to allow that care for ourselves to emerge.

In our own experience with many individuals over many years, healing from the inside out helps make possible the kinds of relationships that people have often yearned for, even outside their prior awareness. We've both seen such healing occur as we've worked with adult children and their parents to help families recover from the disruption that such disconnected relationships can perpetuate across the generations.

Are There Other Ways You're Not Protecting Your Kids?

Setting aside abuse and neglect, there are other forms of ACEs that can affect children and their development. Even if you're confident that you aren't harming your kids in the most extreme ways, consider whether your children might be exposed to threat and fear from more-typical interactions within your family. For instance, sometimes parents deal with intense conflict in front of their kids, screaming at each other and resorting to verbal, emotional, and physical aggression. When a child repeatedly witnesses this type of conflict, and her parents are the source of her fear, it can impair her development of a secure attachment. In fact, recent studies have shown that if a baby's parents are communicating in very angry speech within earshot, even when she is *sleeping,* the baby experiences an increase in neural responses across the parts of her brain that deal with emotion, stress reactivity, and regulation. She experiences threat rather than safety on a physiological level. That doesn't mean that you and your partner should never argue. Conflict is unavoidable and, when done right, even healthy and necessary. But be mindful of your children and pay attention to *how* the adults in the house deal with conflict, and what effects those parental interactions might have on the kids. Parents should protect their children from disrespectful, scary conflict. If you and the other person are too angry to discuss the issue at hand in a safe and civil manner, it's better to wait until you are calm enough or at least away from the children to work through the issue.

Plenty of other experiences, while not leading to disorganized attachment, can prevent our kids from feeling safe in the world. Harm can be done, for example, when kids are exposed to realities they're developmentally unready for. Movies, video games, photographs, and social media all have the potential to harm our children by revealing content or images that they are not ready for, that their young minds can't yet process in healthy ways. Not all media are harmful, obviously, but frightening images, ideas, and themes can overwhelm children, as can sexual content that's inappropriate for their developmental stage, leaving them feeling unsafe and insecure. The same goes for stories told by other kids and older siblings, as well as bullying that they witness, or personally experience, at school.

Without realizing it, parents can make kids feel less safe.

Exposure to scary parental conflict

Becoming scary ourselves

Introduction to inappropriate ideas and images

And even when parents don't commit physical violence against their children, they can of course undermine their children's secure attachment if they humiliate, shame, or yell at them, or use fear-based strategies to purposely frighten them for the sake of discipline or eliciting cooperation. Or when they create situations full of tension and anger, as when divorced parents meet to "hand off" the child from one parent to the other and create an interaction full of discord and antagonism. When parents are reactive and angry toward the other parent, criticize the other parent, ask the child to choose or take sides, or use the child as the communicator or translator of negative information between the adults, it can create intense states of stress that the child cannot change or escape. In these cases, instead of trying to establish and reinforce stability when the child needs it most, parents may be unintentionally chipping away at their child's ability to feel settled and safe. Kaitlin's experiences with her father are a good example of how a parent's behavior can destabilize a child's sense of safety.

These kinds of experiences, while usually less extreme than abuse, are common in more families than people realize. And while these stressors may or may not lead to disorganized attachment, they can still activate the threat response and create the antithesis of safety and security. As such, they violate our two fundamental jobs as parents. If you are allowing or creating a fear state in your child instead of being the source of safety, then you're not only doing harm to your child but also undermining the kind of relationship you want.

Becoming Overprotective Is Not the Answer

All that said, sometimes as parents we are so worried that something bad will happen to our children that we try to manage our fears by oppressively overprotecting. Be careful about allowing the pendulum to swing too far in this direction. Kids can handle appropriate freedoms and challenges. Struggling a bit to figure something out while tolerating some frustration and overcoming a difficult obstacle is

Kids can handle appropriate freedoms and challenges. Struggling a bit to figure something out while tolerating some frustration and overcoming a difficult obstacle is how a child learns that he *can* overcome obstacles.

how a child learns that he *can* overcome obstacles. He'll learn what his abilities and capabilities are when he's faced with a difficulty and gets through it. On the other side of the challenge he'll be stronger and more resilient.

The fact is that sometimes good intentions can actually weaken a child's ability to interact with his world.

Tina worked with a young father named Tom in her office a few years ago. He was a single parent who was extremely conscientious and intentional when it came to parenting his three-year-old daughter, Emily. He went to see Tina because Emily had begun showing signs of anxiety. She was uncomfortable eating in public restaurants; she was scared of movie theaters; she was nervous about the trampoline at her gymnastics class. But what scared her the most was the thought of going to school, which would begin in the fall if Tom could find the right preschool.

Tom explained to Tina that he had been meticulously, but unsuccessfully, searching for the best school for Emily. Each week in Tina's office, despite the initial focus of the work, which was to understand his daughter's anxiety and find better ways to help regulate Emily and build skills, he would regale Tina with the travails of touring and researching that week's particular school. He couldn't find the right school because each of them had glaring problems he just couldn't live with. One "smelled too chemically." Another allowed the kids to take chips and other junk food as part of their snack. ("Can you imagine?!") One offered the kids too much outdoor time, especially considering Emily's many allergies. ("If she rolls in the grass she's itchy for the rest of the day!") Still another school was not play-based enough.

The more Tina talked to Tom about his daughter's prospective school and other parenting decisions, the more she realized that Emily's fear and fretfulness weren't the primary issues that needed to be addressed. The crux of the problem was, pretty clearly, Tom's anxiety. It came from a good place, to be sure. He wanted nothing but the best—the healthiest and the cleanest and the safest and the most diverse and the most musically expressive environment—for his daughter. And obviously, there's nothing wrong with honoring your own values and priorities when it comes to selecting a school that's

Instead of rescuing your kids...

Support them while they struggle.

the right fit for your child. But in Tom's apprehension that his daughter's every experience might not be superlative, he was communicating to her his own angst and unease. So what rubbed off on Emily? A belief that school was scary because of its many dangers. A concern that something bad might happen. She became overanxious as well. Rather than feeling the confidence to explore the world around her, she felt it necessary to stay near her father. Instead of giving his daughter the kind of safety that can lead to resilience and strength, Tom was leaving her with a shaky foundation, meaning she was less willing and able to experience new situations that appeared threatening to her.

Another way we overprotect our kids is by feeling the need to rescue them from difficult moments. That's not what we're talking about when we discuss keeping kids safe. In fact, to help our kids feel okay about exploring and interacting with their world, we have to let them struggle sometimes and, yes, even fail. When they're little this might mean holding ourselves back while we watch them grapple with putting a shoe on a foot or opening a yogurt container.

When we resist the urge to rescue kids, or to complete a difficult chore for them, we show them that we believe they can do it, and we let them learn that they can accomplish these tasks on their own. Then they feel safe to do so. But if we always step in and act on their behalf, we deprive them of the opportunity to develop these important abilities.

> When we resist the urge to rescue kids, or to complete a difficult chore for them, we show them that we believe they can do it, and we let them learn that they can accomplish these tasks on their own.

The same goes for older kids. Consider the common experience of feeling left out by peers at school. If your third grader comes home upset because she's been excluded by the girls she wanted to play with, you might be tempted to call the parents of the other girls and ask them to encourage their daughters to be more inclusive. Or if your sixth grader doesn't make the basketball team, you might

Instead of rescuing your kids...

Support them while they struggle.

want to call the coach and explain that your son just had a bad shooting day during tryouts. But that's not what keeping your child safe means. This is a time to let your daughter discover that social relationships can be tough; to let your son understand that sometimes we try hard and still don't succeed.

You're going to show up for your kids emotionally, to be sure, and you may even support them by helping them problem-solve. That's an important step in creating security because they know you are there for them. But that doesn't mean that you prevent or fix all of

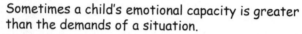

Sometimes a child's emotional capacity is greater than the demands of a situation.

Sometimes the demands of the situation are greater than a child's capacity.

their problems. Instead, you walk beside them through their pain, helping them see that they are strong enough to handle a difficult situation and come out okay. That's how they'll learn to feel safe taking chances.

Obviously, this doesn't mean asking them to do something beyond their capabilities. It all depends on your child's temperament and developmental stage, and on how much stress or change he is already managing at that point in time. A frightened eight-year-old on his first sleepover might need to be picked up in the middle of the night. In other words, that might not be the time to leave him to struggle. Likewise, there might be times you need to step in and advocate for your child if she's having trouble with a teacher. In our book *The Yes Brain* we wrote a whole section about figuring out what kids need from us in various situations, either pushin' or cushion. Sometimes they need pushin' (where we challenge them to do more than they realize they can do), whereas at other times they need some cushion (where we step in to help because they aren't able to handle a situation on their own).

Kids can handle more at some times than at others. Our capacity to deal well with a situation isn't always fixed. Think about your own capacity for patience—some days and moments it's high, and at other times it's low. Same with our kids. In some situations they can handle significant challenge, but at other times they can barely deal with even small obstacles. When the demands of a situation are higher than your child's capacity, she might fall apart or handle it in maladaptive, problematic ways. And when her capacity is higher than the demands of the situation, she will come through in a big way.

So make a distinction between safety and rescue. Find safe ways to let kids wrestle with challenges and even fail. A good example is summer camp. Tina has three boys, and for years all three of them have spent parts of their summers at Camp Chippewa, a boys' adventure and outdoor adventure camp in the Northwoods of Minnesota. One of the many reasons she's such a big believer in the camp experience is that it offers kids the chance to struggle and fail and to face challenges outside of their typical life, but to do so with enough support, encouragement, and fun that they keep working at it. Especially as they move toward adolescence, children feel the need to test their limits. At camp, they can take these risks in nature (and not behind the wheel of a car or at a party) under the watchful eye of responsible adults, proving themselves in positive, nurturing environments that increase their mastery and sense of accomplishment. That means they may be less likely to test themselves in more dangerous, destructive ways at home.

One final word on this subject: As always, keep in mind that kids vary in their tolerance for risk, and in how much they're able or willing to struggle. Some children happily jump in headfirst, and even delight in taking on difficult or new tasks. Others are risk-averse and feel really uncomfortable taking chances or facing an unknown. Remember that every child is different. In each situation, decide what's best for your unique child to keep them safe, while also allowing them to grow and to learn that they can do and be more than they ever imagined.

What You Can Do: Strategies That Promote Feelings of Safety in Your Child

Strategy #1 for Promoting Safety: First, Do No Harm

Our first strategy for promoting feelings of safety in your children is simple, but not always easy to follow: Make a commitment that you won't be the source of fear in your home. Parents can communicate threat in a myriad of ways, and many of them wouldn't be considered abusive. Yelling, threatening, humiliating, spanking, overreacting, and even making certain facial expressions can produce fear in our children. You may never have even considered whether it's okay to use these various forms of expression when you're upset. But having read this chapter, you might want to give some thought to what your kids are experiencing when you become angry or frustrated.

For instance, imagine that you're the parent of a three-year-old who has begun hitting you on a regular basis. He's generally calm at school but has become increasingly aggressive with you, sometimes when you tell him no, and sometimes for seemingly no reason at all. Your automatic physiological and emotional response to the pain is immediate and understandable anger. You want to remain calm and nurturing, but it hurts to be hit, not to mention how frustrating it is that your son is disregarding your instructions not to use violence.

Moments of anger and frustration simply come with being a parent. As far as we know, there's no way around them. And there's not supposed to be. Feelings themselves are good, even healthy. But what we *do* with those feelings can be threatening if we're not careful. What's important is to pay attention to how we act in response to those emotions that arise when our nervous system enters what's called a hyperaroused state. It's not easy to provide the Four S's when we ourselves feel out of control emotionally. The reason is that in those moments, our nervous system's job is to protect *us,* which usually means either gearing up for battle, running away, or shutting down. Rather than the Four S's, it's the Four F's that get prioritized, as your body prepares to fight, flee, freeze, or faint. And these aren't the responses that will help your children feel safe.

Instead, then, it's important that we as parents pay careful attention when we feel our nervous system entering a state of hyperarousal.

As you feel the sting on your thigh when your three-year-old hits you for the third time this morning, your body sends all kinds of signs to tell you that you're in danger of flipping your lid. Your teeth clench. Your muscles tense up. Your eyes widen. You know the feeling.

It's important that we as parents pay careful attention when we feel our nervous system entering a state of hyperarousal.

In high-emotion situations like this, simply telling yourself to calm down may not be all that effective. Counting to ten is another strategy you've heard, and it might help, but maybe not. These are techniques that begin in the upstairs brain, and for certain people they can prove useful. For most people, though, this "top-down" approach to regaining calm isn't so effective, primarily because the emotions arise in the body and the downstairs brain.

Therefore, many people find it more helpful to take a "bottom-up" approach to help shift their emotions when they're in danger of losing control. They can, for example, take a deep breath, letting the exhale last longer than the inhale. Or they can check their posture, noticing the rigidity that the intense emotional state has produced in their limbs. Some find it calming to put one hand on their chest and one on their stomach, and just be still for a moment. Much has been written about these bottom-up techniques, and there are an infinite number of different strategies. The point is to find a way, as you notice your downstairs brain and nervous system becoming aroused, to attend to your emotions and bring your upstairs brain back to a state of equilibrium so you won't be perceived as a threat by your child.

You can't protect your child from every possible danger. You can do your best to keep them safe, but they'll undergo experiences that cause fear and pain. What you want to avoid is being the source of fear and pain yourself.

Strategy #2 for Promoting Safety: Repair, Repair, Repair!

Despite your efforts to do no harm, at times you will likely act in ways you don't like. There's no such thing as a perfect parent, and you're going to make plenty of mistakes as you spend time with and discipline your kids—just like all of us do. We've talked a lot in this chapter about how harmful certain experiences can be for children, and we hope you'll think carefully about ways you can create a greater sense of safety in your child's world and mind. We also hope you'll think about the times you may have frightened your child with the volume and tone of your voice, your words, a scary-looking face, or by being too rough with their bodies. Anytime we move into a reactive state, particularly if it produces fear in our child, we should repair the relationship as soon as we can.

That's our second suggestion for creating safety and helping build your children's sense of belonging: to realize that when you react to your kids from a threatened brain state, you can still repair the breach in the relationship. In doing so, you can provide your kids with all kinds of valuable experiences—even if you're not acting exactly how you'd like.

When you react to your kids from a threatened brain state, you can still repair the breach in the relationship. In doing so, you can provide your kids with all kinds of valuable experiences—even if you're not acting exactly how you'd like.

We're not talking about abuse or neglect here—just those times when you mess up, as we all do. Perhaps you even "flip your lid" in the moment and become so completely driven by reactivity that you lose touch with your receptive, integrative "upstairs brain." In that moment you might declare something ridiculous and call out, a good bit louder than you need to, "That's it! The next time someone complains about where they're sitting in the car, I'm gonna make them sleep in the back seat for the next week!" Or maybe, when your nine-year-old pouts all the way to school because you made her practice her piano, your parting words are, "I hope you have a great day, now that you've ruined my whole morning!"

Clearly, these aren't examples of stellar parenting. But they are common, and we can put them out in the open so we can name them and learn to reduce their frequency and intensity in our relationships with our kids. Flipping our lids occurs when we're upset, and sometimes even when we're not aware of what's going on. That reactive state of fight-flight-freeze-faint can arise rapidly when we feel threatened. This "no-brain" state shuts down our ability to be open and receptive to what's going on in ourselves and in our child. And ironically, when we lose our cool, we can intensify that distress in our child that may have evoked our reactivity in the first place. Without the benefit of your own reflective upstairs brain, you can continue to parent from this reactive, no-brain state without realizing you need to make a repair—inside yourself first, and then with your child. And if you're like most caring parents, you may be hard on yourself when you don't handle things as you feel you should.

So here's hope: Those flipped-lid parenting moments, when repaired, are not necessarily such bad things for your kids to go through. Reducing their frequency and intensity is essential, and reliable repair is crucial. But the truth is, even your mistakes can be used to build kids' feelings of safety and strengthen the parent–child bond.

How? Because these less-than-perfect parental reactions give kids opportunities to deal with difficult situations and therefore develop new skills—like learning to control themselves even though their parent isn't doing such a great job of controlling herself. And then they get to see you come back later and apologize and repair with them. They also learn to tolerate that there are ruptures and then repairs in relationships. But as long as you take steps afterward to restore the relationship and respond effectively there in the moment, you can cut yourself some slack and know that even though you might wish you'd done things differently, the experience was still valuable for your child.

We want to say again: Abuse or even severely harsh parenting is of course different. Or if you're significantly harming the relationship, failing to protect your child, or scaring or hurting them, then the experience is obviously no longer valuable for either of you. In fact, in those cases it's really important to get the help you and your child

need to change the way things happen in your home and allow you both to heal from these woundings. But if you've simply handled a situation poorly, like many of us do, then you can use such a moment to create something instructive and meaningful in your relationship with your child. The postconflict step of repairing the relational breach is crucial. After you've messed up, remind yourself of what matters most—your relationship with your child—and make things right with her.

After you've messed up, remind yourself of what matters most—your relationship with your child—and make things right with her.

Apologize if necessary. Laugh together. The sooner she knows that everything's back to normal between you two, the quicker the relationship can begin to grow and deepen again. And the sooner she will feel safe, knowing that strong feelings won't rupture the relationship long-term. This act of repair will communicate to your child, "Things may get tough between us, but you can't lose my love. I will be here for you. Always and no matter what."

Strategy #3 for Promoting Safety: Help Your Kids Feel Snug in a Safe Harbor

Our final strategy for promoting safety is to create for your children the experience of being "snug in a safe harbor." Even though you're going to make mistakes and overreact to situations at times, you can still create within your home an overall environment of safety and well-being for your kids.

> Even though you're going to make mistakes and overreact to situations at times, you can still create within your home an overall environment of safety and well-being for your kids.

Think of it this way. Before a ship sets out for a voyage at sea, it must establish its seaworthiness by strengthening its hull, fastening its sails, and filling itself with supplies. That preparation takes place in the setting of a safe harbor that protects it from the dangers of the unpredictable and stormy seas that await it on the journey ahead. The enclosed nature of the harbor ensures that the ship is safe, protected from the outer world.

You are the safe harbor for your child.

Though occasional storms of parental distress that create fear and confusion for a child are inevitable, you as a parent can teach your

Be the safe harbor your kids can run to.

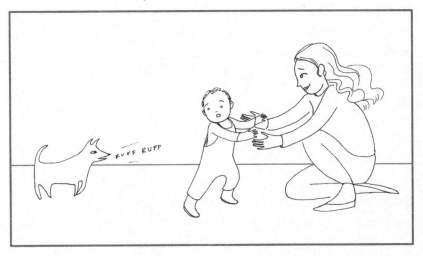

child to weather these storms by creating emotional closeness and reflective communication through open conversations. When a boat at sea is battered by a storm, it seeks a safe harbor to return to in order to make repairs, resupply its food and water, and prepare for the next venture. By having reflective conversations and acknowledging uncomfortable states like fear or confusion so kids make sense of them, you will be teaching your children that you are that safe harbor they can return to again and again to regroup and regain the calmness and clarity to go out into the world. You represent that safety.

Feeling snug in a safe harbor is the experience to keep in mind for your child as you choose how to respond to a given state she is experiencing. If you have a hard time with distressing feelings, your child will learn that you are not a source for being soothed or seen, the next two S's we'll explore, and it will be hard for her to develop the fourth S, an overall state of attachment security. Being a safe harbor means that when a child feels fear from any source—whether the outside world or your own inadvertent scary behavior—you engage your protective mode of being for your child. If you are the cause of a rupture, repair is crucial. But in this third strategy you are creating a safe harbor by the reliable, repeated patterns of communication through which you essentially say to your child, "Whatever the source of your distress or fear, you can rely on me for a safe harbor to protect you from the terrifying storms of life."

Showing Up for Ourselves

At the end of this and each subsequent chapter, we want to give you a chance to process what you've read and apply it not only to your kids and your relationship with them, but also to yourself as an individual. It's obviously important that we promote healthy child-parent attachment, but as we explained in the previous chapter, it's also essential that we reflect on our experiences with our own caregivers.

Reading the opening chapters of this book may have produced gratitude as you thought about the secure attachment you received from your parent or parents. If they gifted you in that way, then showing up for your kids and helping them feel safe will be much easier and probably even feel fairly natural.

On the other hand, if as a child you weren't given the experiences that promote a secure attachment, reading these pages may have been difficult. If you had caregivers who were the source of your terror and/or who didn't protect you when you were frightened, then you might be coming to terms with how hard that was for you. You might be thinking about and understanding why it's difficult for you now to provide those experiences for your kids. In this chapter, we've focused on safety as one of the S's that help move a child toward secure attachment. As we go forward, you'll see how all of these S's are interrelated. You may find that one, two, or all three were absent from or challenging in your childhood. We'll discuss how that impacted your development and may now be influencing your relationship with your child.

It's all the more important, then, that you take time to reflect not only on your experiences with and desires for your own kids, and on the science and philosophy behind the work described here, but also on your early experiences with your own caregivers. Then you can get clearer on where you are now, and thus be a better parent for your kids—one who provides them with the safety and security that prepares them to go out in the world.

With that in mind, look back at the attachment categories in the previous chapter and think about your experiences with your own parents, especially in terms of your feelings of safety. Was your relationship with your parents more like the avoidant form of attachment leading to the adult dismissing strategy? If so, it's likely that you didn't feel encouraged to ask for help or to share your feelings and may have learned to hide them, even from yourself. Or if your attachment relationship with your parents was more like what's called ambivalent, which can lead to a preoccupied adult attachment strategy, then emotional and relational connection and calming were probably not reliably present and at times even intrusive and confusing. You had to remain on edge in your connections with others, uncertain about the relationship and when your needs in that relationship might be met. Or if your attachment experiences with your parents were a further step away from security, they may have created the chaos and unpredictability that comes with the disorganized attachment relationship. Then even your most basic relational interactions might at times have been disorienting and filled with a sense of terror that you could not resolve. Definitely a violation of the fundamental need for safety.

Here are a few questions to help you get clearer on those experiences, and how they might be playing out now that you're a parent:

> Take time to reflect not only on your experiences with and desires for your own kids, and on the science and philosophy behind the work described here, but also on your early experiences with your own caregivers. Then you can get clearer on where you are now, and thus be a better parent for your kids—one who provides them with the safety and security that prepares them to go out in the world.

1. In what ways did your parents or other caregivers help you feel safe? In what ways did you not feel safe? Think about your physical, emotional, and relational experiences.

2. Did you feel protected by your parents? In what ways did they do a good job of protecting you? In what ways did they fail?

3. Did you ever feel terrified of your parents? Were your parents ever the source of your fear?

4. How do you wish your parents had responded differently? What would have been ideal for you to feel safe?

5. Was there anyone you could turn to in your family, or beyond, as a sanctuary of safety?

6. When you think about your child feeling scared by your own parental behavior and reactivity, how does that make you feel? Under what circumstances do you find yourself "flipping your lid"?

7. How do you think your child would want you to respond when he or she comes to you feeling upset after a difficult interaction with you? What could you change?

8. How did repair happen in your family after a subtle or severe rupture when you were growing up? How do you initiate repair now as a parent?

We realize that asking yourself these questions can be challenging and call up all kinds of emotions: guilt, fear, anxiety, sadness, and other feelings, including a longing that's hard to describe, or a state of helplessness or shame. But don't forget the good news for all adults who received less-than-optimal parenting in their youth: You can earn secure attachment by learning about these important ingredients of security and creating them in your life now. By getting clear on your own experiences, and developing a coherent narrative about them—making sense of what happened to you and how it influenced your development—you can earn the type of attachment approach that allows you to learn how to parent in ways that are completely different from, and much healthier than, the ways you were raised.

That's what the carefully conducted research reveals: The attachment strategies we learn as children are open to growth and development throughout the life span.

It can be very helpful to work toward reflection and understanding with a therapist, especially one who is attachment-savvy. You can then start communicating and interacting with your children in a manner that helps them feel safe, regardless of how you were parented. Then, those positive experiences you give your kids will wire their brains in constructive, integrative ways so they can develop into secure, independent, and resilient adults. You can become the safe harbor for your own children that you never had as a child. What's more, as your children grow into adults with secure attachment and a solid emotional base, think of the kind of parents they'll be!

Isn't that thrilling? Because of your courage, hard work, and willingness to reflect on your history and get clear on your own story, you can break an insecure parenting cycle and start a new approach that will strengthen the attachment and cultivate security for your kids and your grandkids, on down through future generations. Showing up for yourself, then, is simply one more way of showing up for your kids, and for their children and grandchildren.

> The attachment strategies we learn as children are open to growth and development throughout the life span.

> As your children grow into adults with secure attachment and a solid emotional base, think of the kind of parents they'll be! Showing up for yourself is simply one more way of showing up for your kids, and for their children and grandchildren.

Seen

CHAPTER 4

The Value of Being Known
Helping Your Kids Feel SEEN

The second of the Four S's is helping kids feel *seen*. At its essence, truly seeing our kids is about three main things: (1) attuning to their internal mental state in a way that lets them know that we *get* them, so they can "feel felt" and understood on a profound and meaningful level; (2) coming to understand their inner life by using our imagination to make sense of what is actually going on inside their mind; and (3) responding in what's called a "contingent" way, where we respond to what we see in a timely and effective manner. Contingent communication depends on a three-step process— perceiving, making sense, and responding in this connecting, timely way—and represents a universal "triad of connection" that helps children feel felt by their caregivers. "Seeing" children in this way means focusing less on a child's specific behavior or the external observable events of a situation, and more on the mind *beneath* the behavior, or what's happening inside.

The old platitude about a relationship needing quality time is absolutely correct. Quantity time matters, of course. Our kids need us to be around, to play with them, to show up at their games and recitals. But helping our kids feel *seen* is about more than just being pres-

the TRIAD of CONNECTION HELPS KIDS FEEL SEEN

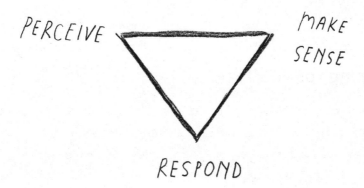

ent physically. It's also about connecting with them in this contingent way—using the triad of connection—and being there when they hurt, as well as celebrating with them when they achieve and succeed, or when they're simply happy. It's about showing up *with our mental presence.*

How good are you at seeing your kids? We mean really seeing them for who they are—perceiving, making sense, and responding to them in these contingent ways, ways that are timely and effective. This is essentially how your child comes to experience the emotional sensation not only of belonging, of feeling felt, but also of being known. Science suggests—and experience supports—that when we show up for our kids and give them the experience of being seen, they can learn how to see themselves with clarity and honesty. When we know our kids in a direct and truthful way, they learn to know themselves that way, too. Seeing our kids means we ourselves need to learn how to perceive, make sense, and respond from a place of pres-

How good are you at seeing your kids? Really seeing them for who they are? When we show up for our kids and give them the experience of being seen, they can learn how to see themselves with clarity and honesty.

ence, to be open to who they actually are and who they are becoming. Not who we'd like them to be, and not filtered through our own fears or desires. Just look at them, know them, embrace them, and support them as they grow into the fullness of themselves.

Take a moment right now and fast forward, in your mind, to a day in the future when your child, now an adult, looks back and talks about whether he felt *seen* by you. Maybe he's talking to a spouse, or a friend, or a therapist. Someone they would be totally, brutally honest with. Can you imagine the scene in your mind's eye? Perhaps he's holding a cup of coffee, saying, "My mom, she wasn't perfect, but I always knew she loved me just as I was." Or, "My dad was *always* in my corner, even when I got in trouble." Would he say something like that? Or would he end up talking about how his parents always wanted him to be something he wasn't, or didn't take the time to really understand him, or wanted him to act in ways that weren't authentic in order to play a particular role in the family or come across a certain way?

We all know the cliché of the dad who wants his nonsporty son to be an athlete, or the mom who rides her child to make straight A's, regardless of whether the child has the aptitude or inclination to do so. These are examples of parents who fail to see who their kids really are. When these are isolated experiences over the course of a childhood, they aren't likely to make a huge difference—after all, no parent can be attuned 100 percent of the time. But when this pattern is repeated, these situations are likely to produce negative consequences for the child, the parent, and the relationship.

A different example occurred with a family we know. Jasmine is a single mom, and her daughter, Alisia, began complaining of unusual headaches when she was eight years old. She began missing school and other activities. After the pediatrician ran tests and proclaimed that there was nothing wrong with Alisia, Jasmine was at a loss. She wanted to support and believe her daughter—she began taking her to one specialist after another—but when she was repeatedly told that nothing appeared to be wrong, she couldn't help but wonder whether Alisia was making up the pain to get out of doing things she didn't want to do. Some days she let Alisia stay home, and some days she made her go to school or her other activities. The result was consistent conflict in the relationship.

The push-and-pull lasted over months, with Jasmine feeling guilty for not believing her daughter but also trying to make sure she didn't miss out on school and important experiences, and Alisia trying her best to make her mom happy but suffering along the way. Eventually they visited a neuropsychologist, who discovered that Alisia did indeed suffer from a complex and puzzling disorder that manifested in just the type of symptoms she was experiencing. The good news was that the disorder was fairly easily treatable with medicine and a diet change. The bad news was that the young girl had suffered so long without relief; and just as bad, she could tell that her mother sometimes didn't believe her when she conveyed what she was going through. Alisia had been living with both physical and emotional pain.

Jasmine, of course, felt awful about not being more supportive of her daughter. She had tried to remain sympathetic and understanding, and did the best she could with the information she had, but she hadn't known how to *make sense* of the disconnect between what her daughter and the doctors were telling her. Even if her perceiving was open, her understanding was clouded, and thus her responding could only be ineffective. That triad of perceiving, making sense, and responding can form a three-link bridge connecting parents and children so that kids feel seen, but in Jasmine's case the bridge wasn't complete. Plus, she recognized that her own emotions were being triggered by the situation with Alisia; Jasmine's mother had been sick often, and the last thing in the world Jasmine wanted to acknowledge was that her daughter might be dealing with some form of chronic illness. The feeling of helplessness in anyone can cloud the ability to create the triad of connection. Eventually, Jasmine got to the bottom of the problem, even though it didn't all go just as she would have hoped.

This is an example of a parent who did her best to show up for her daughter and truly see what was going on with her child. None of us do this right all the time. Life is hard and complex, and having the *intention* to create clear and consistent connection is the best we can offer—repairing when it doesn't go well, and maintaining the mind-set to show up as best we can as life unfolds. Although Jasmine wasn't able to immediately fix the problem, and even though Alisia didn't feel supported throughout the entire process, by remaining vigilant Jasmine was ultimately able to discover the truth about Alisia's pain. A less intentional parent might have simply accused her daughter of being manipulative and forced her to go to school. But Jasmine eventually came through for Alisia. She wasn't perfect, but she showed up and *saw* her daughter, working to perceive, make sense, and respond however she could. In this case an actual diagnosis appeared. But even if Jasmine had determined that Alisia's symptoms *were* contrived or psychosomatic, her role as a mother still would have been to show up for her daughter and perceive, make sense of, and respond to whatever was causing Alisia to tell her she was feeling that way. Regardless of the situation, the more fully we can *see* our kids, the more lovingly we can respond.

Truly seeing our children is often a hit-or-miss proposition, but making sincere efforts along each step of the triad of connection will give us the best chance for connection and understanding.

We offer this example to make the point that seeing your children doesn't mean being a flawless parent. No one can read their kids' cues perfectly all the time, and even if we try, we'll still miss the mark sometimes. We might feel like we're laughing *with* a child, only to have him perceive that we're laughing *at* his expense. Or we might interpret something one of our kids says as evidence of anxiety and respond accordingly, only to have her offended because she feels like we viewed her as weak or unable to handle a situation. Or circumstances might keep us from actually knowing *how* to respond to what we see, as in the case of Alisia and her mother. The point is that truly seeing our children is often a hit-or-miss proposition, but making sincere efforts along each step of the triad of connection will give us the best chance for connection and understanding.

Mindsight

As she labored to address Alisia's situation, Jasmine was demonstrating what we call "mindsight." If you've read some of our other books you might recognize this term, coined by Dan, which describes a person's ability to see inside his or her own mind, as well as the mind of another. A key aspect of mindsight is awareness, in the sense of paying close attention to what's happening below the surface in a situation. This is what Jasmine worked hard to do with her daughter—to see what was going on with her little girl, while also endeavoring to remain aware of her own childhood experiences that were likely coloring her perspective. That's what mindsight can offer: the ability to know your own mind, as well as the mind of another.

For example, imagine that you and your partner are arguing over a parenting issue. Maybe your partner wants the kids to do more chores, whereas you worry that the children are already too busy, so you don't want to add more responsibilities. As your parental conversation progresses the conflict escalates, until you are both furious. At this moment, mindsight would be a powerful tool to call into practice. For one thing, it would create more self-awareness on your part, helping you pay attention not only to your own opinions and desires, but also to your frustration and anger. You might even notice that past issues—with your partner and maybe even with your own parents—are influencing the way you perceive the discussion. This kind of recognition has a good chance of significantly calming the discord.

What could help even more than directing mindsight inwardly for more *self*-understanding is to use it to consider what's happening in the mind of your partner. Many of the various forces within *you* that have helped heighten the tension in the conversation are likely at work within your partner as well. By seeking to understand the fear or other emotions driving their reaction, and even feeling empathy for this person you care about, you can approach the argument—which can now become more of a discussion—much differently, coming at it more from a position of sensitivity and compassion, rather than defensiveness and judgment. You can still hold firm to your own position in the conversation, but your *approach* when communicating that position has a much greater potential to connect, rather than divide, the two of you. That's the power of mindsight.

Yes, you may have guessed it: The triad of connection works not only for your relationship with your kids, but also for those with your other family members, life partners, and friends. Perceiving, making sense, and responding are a fundamental way we establish caring connections in life.

You can see, then, how powerful mindsight can be in a parent-child relationship. Parents who genuinely work on their mindsight skills generally have children who become securely attached. Suppose your four-year-old becomes apoplectic because you drained the bathtub after he got out and he, for some reason known only to him, wanted the tub to stay full. You might be tempted to argue with him, taking on a logic-based, left-brain-dominant approach and explaining the various reasons we always drain the water after a bath. But as you know, logic and rational discussions aren't usually effective with a distraught preschooler. Your brain's way of approaching the situation as an adult in this moment might be diametrically opposed to his own. Perhaps your son's fantasy life was full of ships and sailors ready to set out on an overnight sea voyage while he would be sleeping, dreaming of the voyage unfolding in his bath, if only the bathwater seas had remained in the tub, not spiraled down that drain—you killed the sailors!

What if, instead of approaching only with your own goals and thoughts, you relied on your mindsight to imagine what might be

Instead of lecturing...

Use mindsight to understand and connect.

going on inside of him? You might think about the fact that your little guy has had an exhausting day, with a soccer game followed by a play date. You might tune in to the story he was telling in the bath of sailors and journeys about to unfold. Then you might just hold him instead of lecturing. You might even ask him why it was so important for the water to stay in the bath. And you might acknowledge his feelings: "You wanted the water to stay in this time? You're upset because you didn't want me to drain it. Is that right?" By connecting first in this way, you'll give yourself a much greater chance of helping him calm down and get ready for bed.

Likewise, if your twelve-year-old is in tears because she can't find the shorts she wants to wear to her friend's party, that may not be the best time to reprimand her for not planning ahead or offer a sermon about organization or not putting her things away. You can address family expectations about laundry and room maintenance later, when she can really listen. At that moment, the best thing you can do is to use your mindsight to notice what she's feeling and recognize that, even though you might think her reaction is overblown, her emotions are very real to her. Then, whether you can help find the missing shorts or not, you can at least be aware of your daughter's state of mind at the moment, meaning you can show up for her and help her deal with the disconcerting situation, even if you can't fix the problem itself. Again, showing up for your kids isn't about sheltering them from every problem—you don't need to run to Target to replace the shorts. Showing up is about being there with your children as they learn to manage whatever obstacles they face.

Notice that we're not describing some kind of superparent here. You don't have to be able to read minds or transcend all your shortcomings or achieve some sort of spiritual enlightenment. You just have to show up. Show up *with presence*, and with the intention to let your kids feel that you get them and that you'll be there for them, no matter what. That's what it means to see—really see—your child.

Notice that we're not describing some kind of superparent

Instead of lecturing...

Use mindsight to understand and connect.

here. You don't have to be able to read minds or transcend all your shortcomings or achieve some sort of spiritual enlightenment. You just have to show up. Show up *with presence,* and with the intention to let your kids feel that you get them and that you'll be there for them, no matter what. That's what it means to see—really see—your child.

And remember: It's important to see your own mind as well. That means recognizing how you're feeling at the moment and where your various emotions might be coming from. After all, some of what you experience in the middle of conflict or tension might have nothing to do with your son's bath time, or what your daughter will wear to the party. If you can pay attention to what's happening in your own mind, and with your own emotions, you'll have a much better chance of handling yourself in a way that feels good to both you and your kids. Then, when you're actually *choosing* how you respond in a challenging situation, rather than just *reacting* from your unconscious desires and inclinations, you can really see your kids and respond in a way that provides just what they need in that moment.

What's more, when you respond with mindsight, you'll be teaching your kids how loving relationships work. Attuning, helping a person feel felt, is the basis of a healthy relationship. When we do it for our kids, we're another step closer to developing a secure base. And not only that—our kids will learn how to find friends and partners who will show up for them, as well as how to do the same for others. This means they'll build skills for healthy relationships, including with their own kids, who can then pass the lesson on down the line through future generations.

What Happens When a Child Does Not Feel Seen?

Here's a heartbreaking reality: Some kids live most of their childhood not being seen. Never feeling understood. Imagine how these children feel. When they think about their teachers, their peers, even their parents, one thought runs through their minds: "They don't get me at all."

What keeps a child from feeling seen and understood? Sometimes, it's because we see the child through a "lens" that has more to do with our own desires, fears, and issues than with our child's individual personality, passions, and behavior. That fixed filter can make it difficult for us to perceive, make sense of, and then respond in an

attuned manner. Maybe we become fixated on a label and say, "He's the baby," or "She's the athletic (or shy or artistic) one." Or "He's just like me, a pleaser," or "She's stubborn, just like her dad." When we define our kids like this, using labels or comparisons—or sometimes even diagnoses—to capture and categorize them, we prevent ourselves from really seeing them in the totality of who they are. Yes, we are human and our brains organize the incoming streams of energy flow as concepts and categories. It's just what our brains do. But part of our challenge is to identify such categories and liberate our own minds from their often constraining impact on how we see our child.

For example, "lazy" is a word we hear lots of parents use about their kids. Sometimes it's because a child won't study enough, or practice enough, or willingly help around the house. These parents likely think of "laziness" as a character flaw. But the reality is that when our children exert less effort than we expect or desire, there may be good reasons we haven't thought of that they aren't responding to a situation the way we'd like. Your daughter might be struggling with memorizing the state capitals not because she's lazy, but

Instead of labeling based on assumptions...

Look beneath the surface and ask what's really going on.

because she has a learning challenge that needs to be addressed (in fact, challenged kids are often the ones giving *more* effort than most of their peers, but they're not getting good results and the parents think they need to try harder). Or maybe she hasn't yet learned *how* to study effectively, or she's not getting enough sleep to sustain the energy needed to be alert and to learn well.

Or your son might not be eager to practice his free throw shooting every day because it's not developmentally typical for a ten-year-old to make that kind of commitment to a sport. The point is *not* that your son shouldn't practice if he wants to get better at basketball. Nor is it that your daughter doesn't need to prepare for her geography quiz. We're simply saying that as parents we should avoid making a snap judgment and slapping a label like "lazy" on our kids, rather than pausing to consider what might be going on beneath the surface. Labels can block us from seeing our children clearly. Even worse, our kids pick up on our use of these categories and classifications, then fashion their own self-beliefs around how they think we see them. All of us learn about ourselves through the mirror of the categories others place us in.

A related trap even well-meaning parents can fall into is wanting kids to be something other than who they really are. We might *want* our child to be studious or athletic or artistic or neat or achievement-oriented or something else. But what if he just doesn't care about kicking a ball into a net? Or is unable to do so? What if she has no interest in playing the flute? What if it doesn't seem important to get straight A's, or it feels inauthentic to conform to gender norms?

Each child is an individual. When we let our own desires and categories color our perceptions, then we fail to see them clearly. And if we can't see our kids, then what do we

> As parents we should avoid making a snap judgment and slapping a label like "lazy" on our kids, rather than pausing to consider what might be going on beneath the surface. Labels can block us from seeing our children clearly.

> Each child is an individual. When we let our own desires and categories color our perceptions, then we fail to see them clearly. And if we can't see our kids, then what do we really mean when we say we love them? How can we embrace them for who they really are?

really mean when we say we love them? How can we embrace them for who they really are?

Sometimes the problem is as simple as a lack of fit between parent and child personalities. You might like to move like a hummingbird, accomplishing all tasks in a brisk and efficient manner. Then your daughter comes along with a built-in, inborn pace that's more sloth-speed. Perhaps she's easily distracted. Maybe she's just curious, wanting to explore and learn from the fascinating details that surround her. What's your job there? Is it to mold her into a smaller version of yourself, since efficiency is clearly superior to dilly-dallying? Obviously not. Rather, you might need to make some adjustments to the way you typically handle tasks. Maybe you wake her earlier since she takes longer to get ready for school. Or when you read with her before bed, you might need to allow time for questions and distractions. These are fairly simple modifications, but if you aren't truly seeing her and how she functions in the world, then you won't know her well enough to see how best to alter the routine to make life easier for both of you.

One of the worst ways we can fail to see our children is to ignore their feelings. With a toddler that might mean telling him, as he cries after a fall, "Don't cry. You're not hurt." Or an older child might feel genuinely anxious about something that wouldn't bother you at all, like attending the first meeting of a dance class. It's unlikely that she will feel more at ease if you tell her, "Don't worry about it—there's no reason to be nervous." Yes, we want to reassure our kids, and to be there for them to let them know they'll be okay. But that's far different from denying what they're feeling, and explicitly telling them not to trust their emotions.

So instead, we want to simply see them. Notice what they're experiencing, then be there for them and with them. The words might even be similar. We might end up saying something like, "You're going to be okay," or "Lots of people feel nervous on the first day. I'll be there until you feel comfortable." But if we begin by seeing them and paying attention to what they're feeling, our response will be much more compassionate. Then, when they feel felt, it can create a sense of belonging as your child feels authentically known by you. She will also derive a sense of being both a "me" who is seen and respected, and part of a "we"—something that's bigger than her solo self but that doesn't require a compromise or the loss of her sense of being a unique individual. This is how seeing your child sets the foundation for such future integration in relationships where they can be an individual who is also a part of a connection.

What's more, that empathy we communicate will be much more likely to create calm within our child. As is so often the case, when we show love and support, it makes life better not only for our child but for us as parents as well.

Instead of denying feelings...

See your child and respond.

Welcoming the Fullness of Who Our Kids Are

In previous chapters we've talked about what creates secure attachment. Truly seeing our kids helps establish security since it lets them feel that someone embraces them for who they are—both the good and the bad. We want to communicate to our kids that we welcome them, that we adore them, that we want to know all parts of them, even when those parts aren't always attractive or pleasant or logical. And how do we give our kids that message? In our responses to how they feel or act. Every parent-child interaction sends a message. We give our kids cues as to how we feel about that interaction. And you'd better believe they can read those cues like a card shark reading the room. They know what we're feeling, whether we explicitly state it or not. And the extent to which they feel emotionally secure comes from how well their own inner experiences match with what they pick up from us, as well as how well they learn to make sense of those experiences with our help.

You've experienced this over and over again, even from the time your children were infants. When your baby saw a new person enter the room, or tripped and fell, he immediately looked to you for a signal as to how to respond. He wanted to know, *Should I be afraid right now? Am I safe?* And based on how you reacted, he learned how to gauge his own reaction—both in his behavior and in how his emotions were shaped and expressed. This interaction is called "social referencing," and it represents the very beginning of your child's development into an emotionally aware human. He's *seeing* you.

As he got older, he continued to study you, and he got better and better at reading cues to discover how you felt in a given situation—cues you gave on purpose as explicit communication, or implicit messages embedded in your demeanor that you may not even have known you were sending. And these repeated patterns in communication significantly influenced his own mental model of how to feel about himself and the world around him.

We have friends whose son, Jamie, when he was a year old and climbing or doing something challenging, would audibly, and adorably, tell himself, "Careful, Jamie. Careful." He had internalized and then would mimic the way his parents signaled to him to be more cautious when trying something risky. The cues we give our kids, typically from our own internal signals, can impact them negatively

Instead of denying feelings...

See your child and respond.

or positively. What we communicate can inhibit our kids from exploring in developmentally healthy ways, fueling fear and inappropriate anxiety, or it can stoke courage and the resilience that helps them feel comfortable launching beyond the familiar. (As always, keep inborn temperament in mind. Some kids need to be reminded to be careful, while others need time and encouragement before venturing into unknown realms.)

The point is that our kids learn to interpret fairly precisely how we feel not only about how safe the world at large is, but also how we feel when they communicate their emotions. They might get the repeated message that we truly see them and want to know how they feel—including when their feelings are negative or even scary—and that we will show up emotionally, regardless of how they feel. Or, maybe we communicate just the opposite.

Think for a minute right now about a time your child came to you upset about something. Did you use your mindsight to really see him and offer a contingent response? Which of these responses did you offer, either explicitly or implicitly?

A huge part of building secure attachment is seeing your kids and welcoming the fullness of who they are. It's about making them feel free to share their feelings, even the big and scary ones that threaten to overwhelm them. Remember, they will internalize the messages you send, so if you tell them or give them the feeling that you "don't want to hear it," that will become part of what they know about their relationship with you. This is particularly true when they're struggling, when the stakes are high, or when, as teenagers, they become more private—then you may not hear about things that would be important for them to come to you with. But it's not too late to start communicating to your children that you are there for them. And you can apologize when you fail to do so, then keep sending cues that say how much you love them, regardless of how they act or what they say to you.

Seen versus Shamed

You may have noticed that helping kids feel seen overlaps in certain ways with the experience of safety, the first of our Four S's. We want our kids to feel safe enough to show us who they are, to share with us what they're feeling and experiencing without worrying that we'll react in ways that evoke humiliation and shame, or fear and terror. Then we can see them that much more fully. But they can't show us who they are if they don't feel safe doing so.

For example, if a mother shames her son for being afraid—of being alone, of Halloween costumes, or anything else—then he's not going to let her know when he's feeling anxious. It will therefore be that much more difficult for her to really see him.

As a result, he's left to handle the feelings by himself. From there the problem snowballs. When he gets nervous about going on his first sleepover, he'll be reluctant to tell his mother about his actual feelings. He will be left to face the situation alone, which often leads to more anxiety. So let's say he refuses to go. Maybe he pretends to be sick, or maybe he simply throws a fit and insists he won't go. His mom then sees his actions as oppositional and punishes him, but she never actually sees what's going on within him. If instead she had used her mindsight to simply look and understand, she could have welcomed him to communicate his fear and anxiety. Then he could have shared what he was feeling, and maybe she could even have helped him deal with his nervousness in a way that allowed him to attend the sleepover.

When we dismiss or minimize or blame or shame our kids because of their emotions, we prevent them from showing us who they are.

Shame powerfully impedes the act of seeing. But we do it *so* often with our children. Instead of seeing and connecting with them, then problem-solving and supporting them so they can effectively handle their feelings, we play the shame card. Shame can be direct and involve statements that are dismissive and, if coupled with anger, even humiliating for a child. Shame can also be indirect. This can happen when a child is in an emotionally intense state and we do not attune in that emotional moment even though he or she is making an effort to connect. Repeated disconnection can happen at moments of either a positive state (like excitement about something) or a negative state (such as sadness, anger, or fear) that is not attuned to by the parent and can indirectly create a shame state in the child, or in anyone! Here, at moments of needing connection, none arises. For the developing child who is repeatedly not seen, made sense of, and responded to in an open and effective manner—the triad of connection is not offered at a time of need—these repeated experiences can create a state of shame that comes along with an internal sense that the self is defective. Why? It is, ironically, "safer" to believe that the reason your needs are not being met is because there is something wrong with you, rather than that your parents—whom you depend on for your very survival—are actually not dependable. This is how shame differs from guilt in which there is a sense that a behavior was wrong and can be corrected in the future.

With direct or indirect forms of shaming, we may make our kids feel like they are damaged, that something is wrong with them, even

> When we dismiss or minimize or blame or shame our kids because of their emotions, we prevent them from showing us who they are.

though they are simply being themselves and expressing healthy needs for connection. Sadly, such shame states can remain with us long past our childhood and shape how we function as adults, even if we are not aware that shame is a part of how our lives are being organized.

You can see the difference in the illustrations on the following page. Whereas seeing helps kids calm down and invites them to open up to us, shaming *discourages* them from showing us their true selves. And, worse, the shame typically doesn't even produce the behavior we're looking for. Or, if it does, the child behaves as we want on the outside but does so flooded with fear and dejection on the inside. In fact, research shows that a frequent experience of shame during childhood correlates with a significantly higher likelihood of anxiety, depression, and other mental health challenges.

Of course there are times when we need to challenge our kids to do more than they realize they can do. We don't want them to miss out on the fun of a water slide simply because they're nervous, or to skip a whole soccer season because they feel anxious about going to the first practice. That's not what it means to see and support them. Likewise, we want to be realistic. Seeing a child means being aware of both strengths and weaknesses. So when you observe skills your child needs to work on—whether it's patience, manners, impulse control, empathy, or something else—the loving thing to do is to give them practice in those areas. You don't do them any favors by ignoring who they are, including any shortcomings or obstacles they may face.

But encouraging our kids to step outside their comfort zone, or working with them on social or emotional skills they're lacking, is very different from shaming them when they don't act the way we want. Again, this isn't about coddling them or never asking them to try something new or go beyond what feels comfortable. The point is to allow them to show us what they're really feeling, so we can be present to their experience and help them deal with the big emotions threatening to take them over. It's about seeing them for who they really are.

Shaming our kids prevents them from showing us
who they really are.

SHAMING   SEEING

What You Can Do: Strategies That Help Your Kids Feel Seen

Strategy #1 for Helping Your Kids Feel Seen: Let Your Curiosity Lead You to Take a Deeper Dive

A practical first step to helping our kids feel seen is simply to observe them—just take the time to look at their behavior, attempting to discard preconceived ideas, and consider what's really going on instead of making snap judgments. We can learn a great deal about our kids simply by slowing down and observing them. Seeing openly is made more likely when we challenge categories of understanding.

But again, really seeing our children often requires more than just paying attention to what's readily visible on the surface. Sometimes we have to take a deeper dive to see what's taking place *beneath* the external world of their actions and behavior. We want to observe their activities and listen to what they tell us, for sure. But just as with adults, it's often the case with children that there's more going on beneath the surface than they let on. As parents, then, part of our responsibility is to dive deeper, below what seems obvious.

Practically speaking, that means being willing to look beyond your initial assumptions and interpretations about what's going on with your kids. It means taking an attitude of curiosity rather than immediate judgment.

Diving deeper means being willing to look beyond your initial assumptions and interpretations about what's going on with your kids. It means taking an attitude of curiosity rather than immediate judgment.

This curiosity is key. It's one of the most important tools a caring parent can use. When your toddler plays the "let's push the plate of spaghetti off the high chair" game, your initial response might be frustration. If you assume he's trying to press your buttons or be oppositional in some way, you'll respond accordingly. But if you look at his face and notice how fascinated he is by the red splatter on the floor and the wall, you might feel and respond differently. The cognitive scientists Alison Gopnik, Andrew Meltzoff, and Patricia

Instead of immediately assuming and judging...

Be curious and take a deeper dive.

Kuhl have written about "the scientist in the crib," explaining that a large percentage of what babies and young children do is part of an instinctual drive to learn and explore. So if you're aware of this drive, when the spaghetti splatters, you might be just as frustrated about having to clean it up. But if you can take a moment and give sway to your curiosity, you might pause and ask yourself, "I wonder why he

What we observe:

What the child would say if he were able:

did that?" Then if you see him as a young researcher who is gathering data as he explores this world that's so new to him, you can at the very least respond to his actions with intentionality and patience, even as you clean up the remains of his experiment. (And yes, having gathered your own data regarding this phase your young son is in, you'll know that you likely need to put a towel down the next time you serve pasta.)

In our book *No-Drama Discipline* we encourage parents to "chase the why" behind kids' behavior. By curiously asking "Why is my child doing that?" rather than immediately labeling an action as "bad behavior," we're much more likely to be able to respond to the action for what it is. Sometimes it really may be a behavior that should be addressed—as we keep saying, children definitely need boundaries, and it's our job to teach them what's okay and what's not. But other times a child's action may come from a developmentally typical place, in which case it should be responded to as such. And regardless, even if the behavior does require discipline (defined as teaching and skill building), we'll be much more effective disciplinarians (teachers) if we can curiously chase the why and determine exactly what's going on in the child's mind and where the behavior came from in the first place.

The same goes for other behaviors. If your child is quiet when she meets an adult and resists speaking up and saying hello, she may not be refusing to be well mannered. She may simply be feeling shy or anxious. Again, that doesn't mean that you don't teach her social skills along the way, or encourage her to learn to speak in situations that are uncomfortable. It just means you want to see her for where she is right now. What are the feelings *behind* the behavior? Chase the why and examine the cause of her reticence; then you can respond more intentionally and effectively.

By the way, we're very much in favor of setting clear, and even high, expectations for kids. They need to learn the value of working hard, and to be encouraged to do more than they realize they're capable of. However, there are also times when, if we dive deeper, we'll discover that we're making unrealistic demands on a child. As parents we definitely want to help our kids be all they can be; but we don't want to ask them to do things that are truly out of reach.

An important question to ask is whether a child *won't* behave, as opposed to whether he *can't*. If he *won't* behave as he's asked, then our response may be very different from a situation where he *can't* sit still or consistently follow directions, because of hyperactive tendencies or developmentally inappropriate expectations or some other reason.

Tina recently had an exchange that made this point well. She was speaking to educators about diving deep and chasing the why when it comes to understanding student behavior. During the Q&A at the end of the presentation, a caring and experienced teacher, Debra, stood and said, "If what you're saying is true, then I have to completely rethink the way I handle discipline in my classroom." Tina asked for details, and Debra explained that she used clothespins with the children's names written on them and moved the clothespins into a "red-light, yellow-light, green-light" chart, where the clothespins were all clipped on the large felt traffic light. Each child began a new day in the green light section of the chart; then if they misbehaved, their clothespin would be moved into the yellow-light section, which was a warning. Subsequent infractions moved them into the red-light part of the chart, which meant that parents were notified of the bad behavior and there were specific consequences, such as losing recess.

The rest of the exchange between Tina and Debra went something like this:

TINA: How effectively is the system working?

DEBRA: Great, with most kids. But not with a couple of the boys in my class.

TINA: So the same couple of names are ending up in the red most of the time?

DEBRA: Yes. One boy's pin has been moved so many times his name has rubbed off.

TINA: For the same types of behavior, over and over?

DEBRA: Definitely.

TINA: Well, just based on that, it sounds like the system isn't really working as an effective behavior management tool. The consequences he's facing from you and from his parents aren't really changing his behavior. What about his classmates? How does his difficult behavior impact them?

DEBRA: His peers are annoyed with him, too. They get tired of him intruding on their space, talking to them when they're working. They also hate all the interruptions where we have to stop our class activities to deal with his behavior.

TINA: So let me say back what I'm hearing. At a developmental moment when having your peers accept and like you is so strong, this boy continues these behaviors despite all the negative feedback he's getting from classmates, and then more negative consequences from his parents, and you?

DEBRA: That's what I'm saying. I need to rethink my system.

TINA: Right. Why, in other words, would he continue to do things that lead to such negative responses from virtually everyone around him? Surely that doesn't feel very good to him. Kids typically don't like getting in trouble over and over again and having peers dislike them repeatedly. Let me ask you something. Would you ever move a child's clothespin into the yellow or red sections for not reading quickly enough if the child had dyslexia?

DEBRA: Of course not. He couldn't help that.

TINA: Of course not. Because you'd know it's not a *choice* that the child is making to purposely avoid doing what's expected. I'm wondering if when we see a child who continues with the same nonproductive behaviors that cause so many problems for him, well, maybe it's not a choice for him, either. Is it possible that it's a *can't*, but it's being treated as a *won't*? Maybe he doesn't have the skills or development yet to handle himself differently. If he had a learning challenge, we'd typically see it from a more curious and generous lens and *support* him to thrive. So why would it be different if the challenges are social or emotional or developmental? And we'd never want to punish a child for something the child can't help.

DEBRA: I'd hate it if someone got mad at me for something that wasn't my fault, and especially if it kept happening in front of my friends, and if I was trying to do better but just couldn't.

TINA: Exactly. And none of this means you let the boy flout classroom rules or continue as a distraction. The behavior, obviously, has to be addressed for his sake and for the learning of the others in the room. But this different lens gives you a better idea of why your current system isn't working with this boy. And with more curiosity and a better understanding of where he is, you can address the behavior from not only a more empathetic perspective, but from one that helps you discipline more proactively and effectively as well. It may require some trial and error using alternative strategies and some creativity and patience to help this boy, but I'd encourage you to work *with* him, reflecting on his behaviors together and seeing what he thinks might help him be successful.

This conversation focused on a school situation, but it makes the "can't versus won't" point well. If your child *can't* behave differently, how do you feel about punishing her for what she can't control? Sometimes a can't is rooted in an underlying obstacle, like a learning challenge or sensory processing disorder or pervasive developmental disorder or chronic sleep deprivation or adjusting to a divorce or a new house, or . . . This doesn't mean the child can't grow or build skills; it just means that right now the demand of the environment exceeds her current capacity. The behavior might be more about where the child is developmentally, and she simply needs more time and problem-solving skills to be more successful. But we can't know whether that's the case unless we dive deep and see what's going on beneath the surface.

Strategy #2 for Helping Your Kids Feel Seen: Make Space and Time to Look and Learn

Notice that *intentionality* is key when it comes to really seeing and knowing our kids. The same goes for our second suggestion. Much about seeing our kids is simply paying attention throughout the day. That's one of the great things about a whole-brain approach to parenting: You don't have to wait for big, serious conversations to do the important work of teaching or learning about your kids. You just have to show up and pay attention—to be present.

That being said, though, *while* you're paying attention throughout the day, you can also make a point to generate opportunities that allow your kids to show you who they are. Sure, you can learn all kinds of things simply by observing them while they live their lives, or by listening as they talk about what struck their attention as they went through their day. But you can also take steps to create space for conversations that will take you deeper into their world so you can learn more about them and see details you might not otherwise be privy to.

Nighttime can be a gold mine when it comes to going deeper with your kids. There's something about the end of the day, when the home gets quiet and the body feels tired, when distractions drop away and defenses are down, that makes us more apt to share our thoughts and memories, our fears and desires. The same goes for kids. When they get still and settled, their questions, reflections, wonderings, and ideas can emerge, especially if you're snuggled in close and not rushing them.

What's required, though, is a bit of effort and planning in terms of the family schedule. Kids need an adequate amount of sleep—we can't stress that enough—so ideally you'll begin bedtime early enough to make time for your usual routine *plus* a few minutes of simple chat or even quiet waiting time to allow your children to talk if they are inclined. We've written elsewhere about the dangers of overscheduling children, and how bedtime rituals and ample sleep can be powerful tools for helping regulate their emotions and behavior. With a bit of forethought, you can schedule a few minutes of connecting time as part of your nighttime routine. When they're not rushed, they might feel inclined to share details of the day and ask questions that help you gain a fuller understanding of what's going on in your child's actual and imaginary worlds.

We know what some of you are thinking: *I don't have one of those kids who naturally and willingly shares what they're thinking and feeling.* We get it. Plus, you don't always know how to get conversations started. The answer to the "How was your day" question seems to inevitably lead to the dreaded answer, "Fine." Aren't you tired of asking that? They're sick of hearing it, too! Imagining a chat time added to your child's bedtime routine might produce the unpleasant image of you and your child silently lying next to each other, both of you waiting for something important to be shared.

We have a few responses to this concern. First of all, keep in mind that the idea is *not* that every evening you'll hear some earth-shattering revelation, or that you two will engage in a deep and uber-meaningful exchange. That's not realistic even between adults, much less with kids. What's more, it's not the goal. Sure, there may be times when more significant conversations take place, but remember that the ultimate aim for such moments is simply to *be present* to your children—to create

> There may be times when more significant conversations take place, but remember that the ultimate aim for such moments is simply to *be present* to your children—to create space and time to get to know them better and to understand them at a deeper level, so you can help them grow into the fullness of who they are.

space and time to get to know them better and to understand them at a deeper level, so you can help them grow into the fullness of who they are.

As for the "How was your day" issue, that question may be more than sufficient to elicit details from your particular child. With some

A parent who is familiar with a child's world can ask much more precise questions.

kids, getting them to talk more at bedtime is the *last* thing a parent wants. In these situations, the parent's job may not be to encourage conversation, but to steer it in more focused and profitable directions, so that the discussion can lead to greater connection and understanding. But if you're one of the many parents with a child who doesn't as eagerly share inner thoughts, then you may need to ask more specific questions. And the more you see and know your child, the easier that will become.

You can find plenty of ideas and even products online or in libraries to encourage more meaningful discussions with your kids. Some offer conversation starters; some give you interesting questions to ask, or ethical dilemmas to consider together. You can use the ideas you find to prime the pump of your parent-child dialogue. It's not always easy, but paying close attention to your children and their world will help generate better questions, and you're much more likely to get better answers than "fine." Plus, keep in mind that truly seeing your kids is about being able to read where they are and notice that at times, they simply don't want to talk. Silence is okay too. Being quiet together, simply breathing, can be intimate and connecting. So don't feel pressure to force conversation when it's not the right time.

We know it can be confusing, trying to determine what to say when, and whether to encourage conversation or let things be quiet. But that's one more great thing that comes with really seeing your kids. When you take the time to fully know them, it becomes that much easier to know when to say what, and when to just let silence exist between you. Just a few minutes of space and time to allow anything to emerge from your child's imagination or her day can be very rewarding—for both of you, and for the relationship.

Again, you'll see plenty just by keeping your eyes open as you and your kids live your lives. But one of the best ways to see your kids— and to help them *feel* seen—is to create the space and time that cultivate opportunities for that kind of vision to take place.

Showing Up for Ourselves

One of our deepest needs as humans is connection—to be seen and therefore known. Being understood by another allows us to know ourselves and to live authentically out of our internal experience.

To what degree have you felt seen and known and understood in your own life? When we aren't able to feel or express our internal experiences, or when no one is present in our internal landscape, we can easily feel alone, perhaps losing access to our own insight, reducing even our ability to know *ourselves* deeply.

If you grew up with a caregiver who modeled being aware of his or her inner life, and who paid attention to and honored your feelings and experiences (without becoming overbearing or intrusive), you likely know what it feels like to be seen and acknowledged, to feel felt and understood in your inner world. And chances are you can also do this fairly well in your own relationships. As a result, you enjoy a certain richness in the way you relate to others, including your children, knowing them in deeper ways. Even when things don't go as you'd like, your relationships can serve as a source of strength and meaning.

When we aren't able to feel or express our internal experiences, or when no one is present in our internal landscape, we can easily feel alone, perhaps losing access to our own insight, reducing even our ability to know *ourselves* deeply.

Many people don't have this advantage. They instead grew up in families where almost all of the attention was focused on external and surface-level experiences: what they did and how they behaved, misbehaved, or achieved. Families like these can have fun with one another and enjoy activities together, but the world within is largely ignored. Dinnertime discussions might cover surface topics like current events, what the dog did, what the neighbor said, or other topics that, while being perfectly acceptable subjects of conversation, are

cut off from the internal experiences of feelings, memories, mean-
ings, and thoughts—the subjective, rich, inner nature of the mind.
Their friendships might be outwardly focused as well. We all tend to
have at least some relationships where we discuss superficial topics,
rarely sharing vulnerabilities, thoughts, feelings, desires, or fears,
and that's fine as long as we also have significant friendships where
we're truly known and deeply know the other.

The degree to which we live on the surface without a deeper understanding of ourselves, our significant others, our children, and
our closest friends often correlates with how seen or unseen we felt
by our attachment figures.

Remember from our earlier discussion of attachment approaches
that in an avoidant attachment pattern, the importance of relationships and feelings is dismissed, ignored, or
minimized. In fact, at one year babies
can already demonstrate the adaptive
strategies of avoidant attachment by
externally ignoring their caregivers
after a brief separation—acting as if
they didn't need them. Such a baby
might feel afraid or sad but have already determined that his caregiver
doesn't respond very well when he ex-
presses these feelings and needs. The baby
then adaptively avoids turning to the caregiver to express himself
and instead learns that he's alone in his emotions.

> The degree to which we live on the surface without a deeper understanding of ourselves, our significant others, our children, and our closest friends often correlates with how seen or unseen we felt by our attachment figures.

Without therapy, reflection, or other relationships that give him a
different experience of relationships, the child with an avoidant attachment to the primary caregiver will likely grow into an adult who
focuses primarily on external matters as well. It's an organized, completely adaptive response to his situation. If you have an emotion or
need, and your caregiver ignores it or dismisses it as unimportant,
turning their attention *away* from your need, then it makes perfect
sense that you would begin to live more from a left-hemisphere-

dominant approach to the world, dismissing your own emotions (and everyone else's) as less than important. When you haven't been seen, the circuitry that allows you to tune into other minds and acquire that type of insight doesn't appear to develop as fully, and you can eventually stop seeing yourself.

> When you haven't been seen, you can eventually stop seeing yourself.

You've certainly had people in your life, your parents or colleagues or partners or friends, who felt uncomfortable seeing and dealing with emotions—yours or their own. Those emotions are often expressed with the nonverbal signals of eye contact, facial expressions, tone of voice, postures, gestures, and the timing and intensity of responses. Those are all expressed and perceived predominantly by the right hemisphere of the brain. If that side of the brain didn't have the nurturing, attuned connections that stimulate its growth, it may be relatively underdeveloped—just waiting for a book like this to invite it to get back into the growth and connecting mode! The brain's ability to grow and develop is never lost.

Let's explore a bit and reflect on your experience with your attachment figures and the degree to which you felt seen, known, understood, and responded to. Then we'll let you consider your relationship with your own children. Ask yourself these questions, paying attention to any thoughts and emotions that arise. *See* yourself and your own responses, taking each question one by one, slowing down to give extra thought to any that spark a stronger reaction within you.

1. To what degree did you feel truly seen by your parents, as we define it here (i.e., they perceived your internal landscape deeply, then offered a response that matched)?

2. Do you currently have relationships in which you have more meaningful conversations, where you discuss matters having to do with your memories, fears, desires, and other facets of your inner life?

3. What about with your kids? Do you interact with them in ways that introduce them to and honor their inner worlds? Do you model what it means to pay attention to your own mind and emotions?

4. How often do they feel truly seen by you? Do they feel like you embrace them for who they truly are, even if it's different from you or your desires for them?

5. Do your kids ever feel shamed for having and expressing their emotions? Do they believe that you'll show up and be there for them, even when they're feeling distressed or behaving at their worst?

6. What's one step you could take right now, today, to do a better job of truly seeing your children and responding to what they need? It might have to do with chasing the "why" when something happens you don't like, or creating space to go deeper. Or maybe you want to do a better job of taking an interest in something they care about.

Remember, nobody's perfect, and every parent is going to miss opportunities to see their children. Plus, it's impossible to fully see and completely understand anyone, including our kids. So you shouldn't feel pressure to rise to some level of parental sainthood. Just take one small step toward making your kids feel more seen and understood than they already do. Enjoy the rewards that come with that step, and then take another. Each new step deepens and strengthens the connection, and prepares your children to do the same in their relationships, all the way through childhood and adolescence and into adulthood.

$\underline{S}$oothed

CHAPTER 5

Presence Joins Us as Part of a Calming Whole
Helping Your Kids Feel SOOTHED

Max was the kind of kid you fell in love with right away. A four-year-old with curly black hair and huge brown eyes behind glasses. Bright, creative, and full of life. One person who wasn't so taken with Max, however, was his teacher at his preschool, Mrs. Breedlove. Max was highly anxious and struggled with impulse control and putting on his emotional brakes. Many teachers love emotionally intense, busy boys and successfully channel their challenges into strengths, delighting in how fun they can be, even if difficult at times. Mrs. Breedlove was not one of those teachers. She was an old-school disciplinarian with little patience for "misbehavior" of any kind. She just could not be present for Max or his energy. Not a great match.

One day Max was intently focused on coloring a picture for his mother when Mrs. Breedlove announced to the class that it was time for recess. As the class lined up, Max continued coloring. His teacher called him by name, but he said, not in his most polite tone, "Just wait!"

Mrs. Breedlove responded as you might expect: "Max, that's not how we talk. It's time to line up right now."

Max simply shook his head and stayed busy with his drawing. His teacher's next response was to go over and grab the crayon out of his hand, at which point Max turned to her and pleaded through his angry tears, "Please, Mrs. Breedlove! Please, I just need a minute!"

The situation continued to escalate. Mrs. Breedlove reached for Max's picture, and he pushed her hand away. She reached again, and when he tried to protect it, it ripped. At that point he exploded and slapped his teacher's leg. "That was for my mom!" he screamed.

Five minutes later he was in the school office, still fuming, still crying, when the school counselor appeared. She could immediately see the fury in his face and posture. She had worked with Max before and knew him fairly well. She also knew a bit about social and emotional development. She sat next to him and put her hand on his shoulder. "Oh, buddy, you're so angry. What happened?"

Max's response, if maybe a bit violent, showed an impressive amount of creativity and forethought for such a little guy. Still seething, he said, "I'm gonna use my magic and turn her into a seed. Then I'm gonna wait for her to grow into a tree. Then when it's tall I'm gonna chop it down and feed it into a wood chipper, then take the wood chips and mix them in with some asphalt, and pour it on the road, and then run over it all with a steamroller!"

The counselor tried not to show how humorous she found this imaginative young lumberjack-streetworker's (really, really) long-term plan for vengeance. She wanted to avoid encouraging any focus on violence, but she was impressed with his creativity and wanted to help him use his inventive powers for good instead of evil. So she spent time calming him so he could regain composure and understand how he could have handled the situation differently. In a few minutes they could engage in a peaceful, productive conversation, where he actually demonstrated remarkable insight about what had unfolded. He just couldn't access that sophisticated part of his brain in the moment when he was so angry.

So what if, in the first place, Mrs. Breedlove had approached the situation by attempting to *comfort* Max, using soothing as a tool to encourage cooperation and problem solving instead of controlling or managing him? What if she had sought to see and understand his mind before the escalation, then realized as he began to get upset that he needed *help* regulating his emotions? He was only four, after all. What if, when he told her to wait, she had gone to his desk and attempted connection, or something that we might call "proactive soothing"? She could have said, "I can tell this picture is important. Who is it for?" Then she could have followed up by telling Max, "I know you love making things for your mom. Hmmm. Since it's time to go outside to play now, where do you think we should put it to make sure it's really safe until you can finish it later? Yes, top of my desk, with my other really important papers. That will protect it while you play outside. Then when we come back in, I'll make sure you have time to finish your drawing for your mom so you can surprise her at pickup." If Mrs. Breedlove could have been present—remaining openly aware and receptive to what was going on, not just in Max's behavior but in his inner life—then a soothing connection could have been established. Max, instead of being alone, would have felt *joined*. Max and his teacher could have become a "we" that would enable his emotions to be soothed as he transitioned from one activity to another. Imagine the difference such an approach would have made, how much time it could have saved, and how it would have affected Max's brain and nervous system, and therefore his emotions and behavior, creating calm and regulation that could have diffused the tension in the interaction.

Imagine the difference such an approach would have made, and how it would have affected his brain and nervous system, and therefore his emotions and behavior, creating calm and regulation that could have diffused the tension in the interaction.

Instead, because of the way the conflict was actually handled, Max's reaction was typical for him, even predictable. He became overwhelmed by his big emotions, which grew and grew until he lost the ability to regulate himself, control his body, and make good decisions. At that moment, naturally, his teacher was even less likely to be present for him. Soothing was the last thing on her mind, and the last thing likely to happen to Max's distress. And since he didn't receive any help in dealing with his big feelings, he internalized a lesson that was reinforced in repeated interactions with his teacher and other adults who expected him to handle his emotions in ways he wasn't yet able to do: *When I get overwhelmed with big feelings, no one is going to help me. In fact, I'm going to get in trouble.* These repeated interactions actually often increase the frequency and intensity of the dysregulation and anxiety. If, on the other hand, the teacher had been present, with open awareness and a receptive approach, it would have soothed him, and his brain could have begun to encode a new model: *If my feelings get big and out of control, someone will be there for me and help me calm down and make good decisions.* These repeated interactions will usually *decrease* the frequency and intensity of the dysregulation and anxiety.

Once Max was calm again, his teacher could still have addressed the difficult behavior and helped him build skills like patience and impulse control. But first he needed help getting calm so his brain could move from reactive to receptive, so he could even *hear* the lessons he needed to learn. The simple act of soothing, and the connection it would lead to, could have changed Max's whole trajectory. He likely would have gone to recess with his friends, rather than sitting in the office devising violent, time-consuming schemes involving horticulture and asphalt. Then with repeated soothing, new expectations and new models could be reinforced in his mind. Instead of being alone, he'd be joined and part of a "we."

We've seen this time and again over the years in our work with schools and families. When adults change *their* behavior in response to a child's intense reactions, it can change the child's behavior. Tina worked with a school district in Texas that embraced a shift from a primarily behavioral approach to a more relational coregulating approach, which we outline in *No-Drama Discipline*. They found that when their most dysregulated, reactive students were given empathy, connection, soothing, and support in the moments they were dysregulated, they calmed down more quickly than the times they were punished for their reactions or were told to go into a room and calm themselves down. And remarkably, but not surprisingly, they found that this soothing approach over time also began significantly decreasing the length, intensity, and frequency of behavioral outbursts and other disciplinary issues.

It makes sense, doesn't it? If you're a child (or even an adult), and your reactive emotions and neurophysiology engulf you, and you know you will ultimately get in trouble for something you can't help, then you'll experience an increased amount of distress, anger, fear, and anxiety. That can be pretty overwhelming. But if instead you know you'll be helped when you become upset, your nervous system doesn't have to get so dialed up. You can bypass the learned feedback loop that comes when your big feelings produce fear and anxiety—more big feelings—simply *because* you find yourself experiencing strong emotions. That negative feedback loop is what can take place in the mind of a child when a caregiver gives her the message, *If you find yourself in a situation where you are overwhelmed and out of control, you will be punished.* Instead, we want them to receive a consistent message of support: *If you find yourself in a situation where you are overwhelmed and out of control, I will help you, and together we'll get you back to calm. You might not get what you want right now, but it will be okay. I'm here for you.*

Soothing comes from joining. And joining comes from our being present. That's how we show up to soothe.

The Goal: Move Toward Inner Soothing

In the previous chapters we've talked about what a difference it can make in the life of a child when she feels *safe* and *seen*. In Max's story you see the power of making sure a child feels *soothed* as well—or what can happen when we don't provide that kind of presence. When a child is in distress—when she's suffering emotionally or her nervous system is sending her into fight, flight, freeze, or faint—that negative state can be shifted by an interaction with a caregiver who shows up for her. She might still suffer, but at least she won't be alone in her pain. The experience will occur in the context of the parental presence, and she'll be attuned to and cared for. From a scientific perspective, that joining even in the face of pain and distress changes the child's experience from one of being alone in her discomfort to being part of a larger whole. That way of joining, the *interpersonal* experience of having someone bear witness to her distress, then being comforted and connected, creates a sense of trust that opens the window to many *inner* mechanisms that heal pain, reduce distress, and build resilience. Inter-soothing is the gateway to personal inner soothing.

Put differently, the repeated experience of *interactive* soothing can lead to an *internalized* capacity for the child to soothe herself when she needs it. When she learns, through experience, that someone will show up for her over and over again when she's hurting, she'll learn how to show up for her inner self, developing the ability to more autonomously soothe and regulate her own emotions. Her caregiver soothes her interpersonally now, thus building the neurological circuits for inner soothing.

The repeated experience of *interactive* soothing leads to an *internalized* capacity to soothe herself when she needs it. In other words, when she learns, through experience, that someone will show up for her over and over again when she's hurting, she'll learn how to show up for her inner self, developing the ability to more autonomously soothe and regulate her own emotions.

The ramifications of building the inner capacity to soothe ourselves are enormous. When a child learns to autonomously help himself calm down in the midst of anger, frustration, disappointment, or anxiety, that's evidence of the growth and development of his prefrontal cortex—the upstairs brain. And what is the upstairs brain in charge of? Some of the skills and capacities we most want our kids to develop:

Soothing a child helps develop the upstairs brain and promotes its more sophisticated functions.

✔ Sound decision-making and planning

✔ Regulating emotions and body

✔ Flexibility and adaptability

✔ Empathy

✔ Self-understanding

✔ Morality

In other words, when we use connection and relationship to soothe our kids, and they thereby learn to inwardly soothe themselves, we're not only giving them a tool that will help them remain calm in high-stress situations. We're doing that, for sure. But we're also, through the power of neuroplasticity, promoting change within the hardware of their brains that will allow them to develop significantly greater resilience, as well as live fuller and happier lives.

You may notice we are not using some common terms like "self-soothing" or its scientific counterpart, "self-regulation." Instead, we are emphasizing that the experience of "self" has both an *inner* and

THE ANATOMY of INNER SOOTHING

Parent's upstairs brain perceives Child's distress → Parent seeks to join through interpersonal soothing → Child becomes regulated → Growth of Child's upstairs brain is stimulated → Child develops capacity for inner soothing

an *inter* aspect. In this way, the "self" is within us, within our body and its brain, and between us, between our inner selves and the world around us—whether that space between is about our connections with people, like our parents or peers, or with pets and the planet. We can find "inter-soothing" by going outside and breathing in some fresh air, by going out into nature, by petting our dog, by jogging or swimming. This is how our "self" is an interconnected part of others and the planet. As a parent, teaching your child about this "inter" aspect of who they are builds in an important relational sense of their connection to "something more" than just their inner, bodily based self. That something-more gift, as we'll see, gives a deep sense of belonging to a world much larger than the isolated, "me-focused" view that contemporary society so often emphasizes, to the sad isolation and detriment of youth. This is how your own presence gives your child the experience of being a part of a "we" that is the two of you. Your child develops a sense of belonging to something more than just a solo self, of identity as a relational self as well as an inner self.

Plus, as a result of these interactive joining experiences that cultivate those changes in your child's upstairs brain, your job as a parent will become much easier. To see why, just look at the earlier illustration listing the functions of the upstairs brain. Imagine your children

Two Aspects of Soothing the Self
Inner-soothing

Inter-soothing

developing into individuals who regularly display these various skills. Long term, they'll reap the rewards in the form of better relationships, clearer self-understanding, success, and broader overall happiness. And short term, the two of you will enjoy a more harmonious parent-child relationship, since they'll be better at making decisions, controlling their actions, thinking of others, understanding themselves, and behaving in moral and ethical ways. All of this begins with soothing, with what's called dyadic regulation or co-regulation, where you and your child work together as a pair, a dyad, to create more connection and calm so emotions less frequently take over and create havoc.

The goal is inner self-regulation, to be sure, where kids can regulate their inner mind and emotions. But we have to be patient along the way. Development takes time. That means that we co-regulate until our kids can do it for themselves. The upstairs brain isn't fully developed until the midtwenties, so throughout childhood and adolescence—and even into adulthood!—there will be times our children need us to soothe and calm them when they're upset. Just as children and teenagers may need our input when thinking through certain decisions along with the attendant ramifications and risks, they may require support with emotional regulation as well.

Soothing and the Green Zone

One of the best ways to understand the actual mechanism of soothing is to think about zones that represent the intensity of your child's emotions. We explained this model in detail in our book *The Yes Brain*. The basic idea is that under normal circumstances we want our kids to be in the green zone. There they can handle themselves well, feeling safe and in control, even when situations get a bit challenging. But when they get too revved up—because of anger or fear or another uncomfortable emotion that creates the kind of inner chaos that sends them out of control—they enter the red zone, where their nervous system dials things way up. Or, if big emotions force them to shut down and freeze or hide, they enter the blue zone, where their nervous system dials things way down. (The image opposite is black and white, but you get the idea.)

When children leave the green zone, losing control and entering either the chaotic red or the shut-down blue, then they are dysregulated. We can call this state "flipping your lid" because the prefrontal cortex, the upstairs brain, becomes disconnected from the reactive lower parts of the brain that hijack our thoughtful, regulated self. This disconnection is the basis of how the brain in that moment is no longer integrated—the linkage of differentiated parts is temporarily suspended. In that disintegrated state kids need someone, namely you, to step in and co-regulate so they can move back into the harmony of integration and regain control of their emotions, bodies, and decisions.

> When kids have flipped their lids, they need someone, namely you, to step in and co-regulate so they can move back into the harmony of integration and regain control of their emotions, bodies, and decisions.

Imagine, for example, that your toddler has flipped her lid and moved completely into the red zone over something that seems entirely ridiculous. Let's say she wants to climb into the refrigerator and have you close the door so she can see whether the light goes out. Then you show her the button that turns off the light when the door closes, but she continues to insist that she wants to see it from the inside. You refuse to allow her, and despite the empathy you offer as you enforce the boundary, she becomes more and more agitated and begins to melt down. (If you know toddlers, then you know that this is *not* a far-fetched scenario!)

The classic, age-old advice parents often hear is to ignore a tantrum. We're told not to give it any attention; otherwise the toddler can use it as a tool to get what he wants anytime you tell him no. Of course you want to avoid giving in and allowing a child to cross a boundary you've set or do something dangerous simply because he's throwing a fit. But the truth is that, especially with young children, a tantrum is often a moment when the child is truly out of control. Not always, but often, controlling himself might be more of a *can't* than a *won't*. And if a child *can't* regain control once he's become upset, then does it make sense to ignore his tantrum? He may *need* you in that moment in order to regain control.

Recall that dyadic regulation leads to internal regulation. In this way, these co-regulating interactions lead to growth of the child's brain that allows for the development of more autonomous capacities to regulate their internal states. In zone terms, connecting with our children when they are in the blue or red zone and helping guide them back to the green zone is what teaches them how to do this for themselves in the future. This approach to parenting focuses on both creating green zone states now, and building the regulatory circuitry for resilience in the future. That's how we help our kids build skills, not just control their behavior in the moment.

> We want to help our kids build skills, not just control their behavior in the moment.

Plus, regardless of whether your child is really unable to regulate himself and has lost control, with stress hormones and threat signals from his brain and body surging (what we call a downstairs tantrum, based on the part of the brain that's calling the shots in that moment), or is able to control himself but is *choosing* to cry and flail in the hope of getting want he wants (an upstairs tantrum), our response can be the same. Hold the boundary, but do so while providing support and soothing for the emotions and reactions that result. This is a point many parents often miss: We really can hold firm boundaries about behaviors and expectations while being "soft" toward the child and his emotions. Giving in or ignoring the child and his feelings are not our only options! We can connect first, then redirect.

None of this, in other words, means that you clear out your vegetable crisper and your milk and strawberries so there's room for your daughter to climb into your Frigidaire. It simply means that she needs you to soothe her, to co-regulate so she can come back to her senses and re-enter the green zone.

> We really can hold firm boundaries about behaviors and expectations while being "soft" toward the child and his emotions. Giving in or ignoring the child and his feelings are not our only options! We can connect first, then redirect.

By connecting in this way a child can move back into the green. What's more, she will have had the experience of becoming dysregulated and then moving back into regulation with your help. And each time she has that experience, and as her development unfolds, her brain will be wiring to grow stronger and stronger so she'll be able to self-regulate more automatically even when you're not there. These co-regulatory interactions build integration into your child's brain—the basis of her developing inner regulatory skills and resilience.

The same goes for misbehavior. Let's say your nine-year-old becomes so upset with his sister that he throws one of her new walkie-talkies against the wall and breaks it. As he wails in anger, completely out of control, that's not the most effective time to talk to him about respecting personal property or apologizing to his sister. He won't even be able to hear you or process that information in that reactive state, and he's *not* feeling empathy for his sister. In fact, he wishes he'd broken all her things! There will be time to redirect, but first, con-

Instead of ignoring a tantrum...

Soothe your child and help her re-enter the green zone.

nect. When soothing is your initial response, you will help him calm down. Then, once he's back in the green, you can redirect the behavior and talk about making things right with his sister, or possibly saving his allowance to replace the walkie-talkie. You can also much more effectively work with him on any necessary skill building and

Connect and Redirect
First connect, helping them return to the green zone.

Then redirect.

help him come up with a better strategy to handle his anger next time.

We don't mean to make this connect-and-redirect process sound easier than it is. When children go into the red zone like this, or when they run and hide and enter the blue zone where they don't want to talk or interact with you, it can be hard on a parent. But you'll be much more successful teaching better ways to handle circumstances in the future if you can help your upset child calm down first before you begin the instruction. And granted, sometimes your efforts won't be immediately or obviously successful at helping your child return to the green zone. It can take time to calm down and let the nervous system settle. In that case you can simply remain present, staying close by and offering help if he can't calm down on his own, so he knows he's not alone in his emotional distress.

Soothing: All About the Feel

Remember the triad of connection: perceive, make sense, and respond. This response can definitely involve words, especially when they're communicated in a caring, empathic tone. It can be remarkably calming and comforting to hear, "That really hurt, didn't it?" or "I'm here. I'm here." Validating, assuring, identifying, and expressing empathy are all powerful ways to use words to help soothe a child (or an adolescent or even an adult for that matter).

But the vast majority of the soothing process takes place nonverbally. Think about the difference tone of voice can make.

This lesson applies even as kids get older. When you confront your child about something she did, and she reacts by attacking you in her anger and defensiveness, your tone can influence whether she moves further toward reactivity and frustration and the red zone, or back into calm and control and the green zone. If you can help her feel heard and listened to—*I understand, honey. You felt like I blamed you without listening to your side first*—you'll be much better able to stay focused on teaching and skill building around the issue at hand, and produce fewer personal attacks as she lashes out.

Other nonverbal cues—the look on your face, your eye contact, your tone of voice, your posture, the timing and intensity of your response—all offer enormous potential to quell raging emotions.

These nonverbal signals are a central way we connect with one another. Pay attention to how you might be coming across to your kids, even when you say nothing at all.

The power of touch can be especially influential in a situation that calls for soothing. But again, attune to your kids and determine

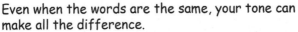

What are you communicating with your nonverbal cues?

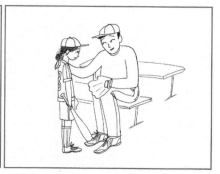

what they need based on who they are as individuals. Some might not find touch soothing at all. For most kids, though, patting or rubbing their back or holding and rocking them while holding their hand can have a powerful effect in terms of helping them return to the green zone.

From the moment they're born, holding small children can do wonders, especially when they're experiencing distress. A recent study found that the amount of comfort and physical contact infants receive affects not only their current emotional state, but their actual molecular profile. Researchers looked at four-year-olds who had experienced a higher-than-typical amount of distress as infants and received less soothing physical touch in response. Results showed that these children, four years later, were behind their peers in terms of biological development. Not only that, the researchers found that these negative effects could actually alter the children's biochemistry and affect genetic expression—the ways their genes were being activated in what's called "epigenetic" regulation. Other studies show that hospitalized babies heal and develop much faster when held. Skin-to-skin contact, as in this kind of "kangaroo care," not only soothes—it literally heals and fosters development. What's more, the neuroscientist James Coan has performed experiments demonstrating that a person anticipating and then receiving a shock will report less anxiety and even physical pain when an attachment figure, in this case a romantic partner, simply holds their hand.

Even as our kids get older, again being respectful of personal preferences, appropriate physical affection should remain in any parent's go-to bag. Tina's twelve-year-old is taller and weighs more than she does, so there's no way she can pick him up and hold him when he's upset (although it would be funny, if not injurious, to see her try). But hugging him, or sitting next to him and putting her arm around him while she rubs his back, can still do the trick in a significant way. The same goes for one of her teenagers, but not for the other one. One welcomes touch and a hug, but when the other one is upset, she knows to just sit close and put her hand on his arm, or possibly an arm around his shoulders. As much as possible, we want to approach each child as an individual, and offer what he or she needs in that particular moment.

Notice, too, how much the other S's come into play when it comes to soothing. For us to co-regulate and help pacify the raging storms of emotion, we must make our kids feel *seen* and understood. And there's no way that can happen unless they first feel *safe* when they turn to us.

What Happens When a Child Does *Not* Feel Soothed?

When a child is in need emotionally and a caregiver offers an attuned and caring response in a timely fashion, that's called a *contingent* response. The caregiver observes and attunes to the child's internal state, makes sense of that inner experience as best she can, and then offers a response that matches. That's the triad of connection. In turn, the child knows that he is understood. The child "feels felt." Not only that, he learns that he can trust his internal experience, and count on his caregiver to *get* him. That's what we saw when the school counselor came across Max, crying and fuming in the school office. Her response was contingent because she attended to his feelings, made sense of them, and responded in a timely and effective manner—"Oh, buddy, you're so angry"—letting him know he was heard and cared for.

A noncontingent response is the opposite. That's what his teacher offered. As he began to enter the red zone when the conflict escalated, Mrs. Breedlove failed to soothe his emotions. Yes, she responded to his *behavior*—"That's not how we talk"—but she didn't pay attention to the *feelings* he was expressing. She never said, "I know it's really important to you to complete the drawing for your mother" or, "I can tell you're worried you won't have enough time. After recess we'll talk about that and let you finish." Since the feelings weren't addressed, the response she offered was noncontingent, and four-year-old Max was left to deal with his big emotions alone. When another is not receptive to our inner world, and doesn't attempt to make sense of that inner experience and respond as best they can in a timely and effective manner, we can feel misunderstood, dismissed, unloved, and invisible. The natural response to such noncontingent communication can be to enter the red zone in anger or the blue zone in despair and dejection.

A noncontingent response from a caregiver fails to match what the child is experiencing, which leaves the child either doubting her own internal experience or the caregiver's ability to "get it" and help.

It does nothing to soothe the child, who has two main options in response to the strong emotions she's experiencing. The first is simply to remain upset and deal with the troubling feelings alone, which often means she becomes even more upset. When the child leaves the green zone and there's no one to help her address the strong emotions, then the nervous system doesn't get the opportunity to return to a place of calm and regulation. Typically, this means that when things don't go her way in the future, the intensity, duration, and frequency of her moments of distress will increase.

You'll remember from chapter 2 that in the Strange Situation research scenario, when babies were separated from their parents, researchers at times witnessed what came to be labeled an ambivalent parent-child attachment. For these children, when the parents returned to the room after a brief separation—what's called the "reunion phase"—the child might show distress and ask for comfort, but the caregiver would not be very successful in soothing the baby. Put another way, the baby was not readily soothed, because at only twelve months of age, the child had already learned from repeated experiences that this parent would likely not be *able* to soothe him. Attachment strategies are evoked with that particular parent, and they involve the child's state dependent memory—images, feelings, and behaviors that are activated in the presence of that particular parent. In this situation, a child might be seen as clingy, unable to settle down and return to play. But the reality is that this is a relational state, not a feature of the child alone. In the presence of another parent with whom the child has had, for example, secure attachment, his behavior will be quite different. How can this be? As we've seen from the beginning of our discussions together, repeated experiences shape the brain's creation of a mental model as it constructs a generalized schema of all the experiences the child has had with that particular individual. Mental models are a part of our state dependent memory system. This attachment mental model is activated with the present moment experience, and in this way might be of security with one parent or insecurity with another. This attachment model that has the pattern of ambivalence develops when the child has experienced repeatedly the parent's typical response as unreliable and the parent is inconsistent at meeting his emotional needs. Sometimes in the past they had shown up for him, and sometimes they hadn't. This behavioral pattern can also include times when the parent is emotionally intrusive, and thus so noncontingent that the parent's own internal state dominates the communication. As we've seen, this could include the experience of a parent's anxiety intruding on a child's fear, intensifying the child's distress instead of soothing it. The model in this case would be one of a confused state of mind. This is why the child feels anxiety and ambivalence about whether the caregiver can be trusted to soothe and help. So in this dynamic—in this state of being with this particular parent with this particular history of interactions—the baby is ultimately not soothed, and remains in emotional distress, unable to quickly return to a state of balance. This is a relational state, not a feature of the child alone at this point in her development.

Another primary response when children experience big emotions, but don't have anyone to reliably help them regulate, is to simply disconnect from their feelings. In the Strange Situation, this results in what attachment researchers call an avoidant attachment response during the reunion. This relational pattern emerges when babies learn that their needs are not going to be addressed in a contingent fashion. In effect, they internalize the reality that when they need soothing, their caregiver doesn't provide it. So, even though their inborn, instinctual need for attachment is still activated, which can be seen in elevated heart rate and other physiological measures of stress, they have adapted to the common response from their caregiver by constructing an attachment model with this parent as one of disconnection, the avoidant attachment pattern. This typically means that they don't show their distress or even request an emotional response from the parent. During the reunion phase, when the parent returns, this baby doesn't seek to reconnect or to be soothed from any distress she might have experienced when her caregiver left the room. And likewise, the caregiver provides none. Little attention is given to the child's internal experience. She simply keeps her focus on the toys and the external world, as does the parent. Here we see that in this relational setting, the attachment strategy is to focus on the world of behaviors and things, not on the internal state of the mind's feelings, thoughts, or memories.

These two attachment strategies from children when their caregivers fail to soothe them—either to remain in emotional distress as in ambivalent attachment, or disconnect from their feelings as in avoidant attachment—can prevent children from developing a rich and rewarding emotional life. It can mean having difficulty seeing their own emotions and then being able to soothe themselves. In a perfect world, all parents would help their children develop secure attachment by providing attuned, sensitive, timely, and predictable care when they are upset. When children reliably have contingent connections, they develop secure attachment. The children who demonstrate secure attachment with their parent in the Strange Situation count on this type of soothing, which is why during the reunion phase they communicate their upset feelings and reach for their caregivers, then become quickly soothed and return to playing. They feel secure that their parent will be there to comfort them the next time they need it. Unfortunately, only a little over half of children receive this kind of consistent, contingent care from their primary caregivers; far too many children don't have this security.

When we talk about soothing children who are having a hard time, even when that manifests as a challenging behavior, parents sometimes assume we're encouraging permissive parenting, where there are few boundaries and parents let their children rule the roost. This is *not* what we're saying.

Soothing Is *Not* the Same Thing as Coddling

Before we turn to some practical suggestions for helping your kids feel soothed and secure, let us reiterate one important point: We are *not* saying to give them everything they want. When we talk about soothing children who are having a hard time, even when that manifests as a challenging behavior, parents sometimes assume we're encouraging permissive parenting, where there are few boundaries and parents let their children rule the roost. This is *not* what we're saying.

If you've read any of our other books, you know that we are big believers in setting clear, firm boundaries for children and even hav-

A world without rules.

Rules provide safety rails.

ing high expectations for them, particularly when it comes to being respectful of themselves and others. The old cliché about kids needing limits is exactly right. A world without rules and boundaries is a world of chaos, which is frightening. Children need to know what's expected of them. They need to know what's okay, and what's not. It helps them feel that the world is predictable and safe.

Plus, kids need to internalize and get used to hearing the word "no." That gives them practice at putting on the brakes and stopping themselves. The world, after all, is certainly not going to tell them yes all the time. And they certainly can't just do whatever they want, whenever they want, without some pretty serious natural consequences.

That being said, though, as you say no to certain behaviors, you can say yes to who your child is and what she's feeling. *Of course* set limits; saying yes to who your child is doesn't mean you should let her throw her fries at the restaurant. It doesn't mean you have to let it

Even as you say no to certain behaviors, say yes to who your child is and what she's feeling.

slide when she hits her baby brother, or speaks disrespectfully to you. It means you're prizing the relationship, *even when* you're addressing misbehavior. Setting boundaries is part of loving our children. But we can do so in a way that communicates love and acceptance, of the child if not the behavior.

Imagine, for instance, you let your seven-year-old stay up later one night because his big brother has friends over. But when it comes time for him to go to bed, he cries and resists. You might be tempted to respond strictly out of your own frustration and say, "I gave you extra time! What are you crying about? You should be glad I gave you an extra thirty minutes. Now go to bed." For good measure, you might even throw in something like, "Next time I won't even give you extra time if you're going to fuss anyway."

Practically every parent has uttered similar phrases in a moment of exasperation. All of us handle situations in ways we don't want to (and that we hope our neighbors don't hear!) when we're annoyed. But notice that the irritated response will likely not only fail to help the child regain composure—he's probably going to go even further into the red zone—but also be completely ineffective when it comes to your primary goal in the moment, getting him to sleep in a timely manner. Now he's going to cry even harder, meaning it will be that much longer before he falls asleep. Plus, bedtime battles often send parents into the red zone as well. Isn't it ironic that we sometimes end up yelling, "GO TO SLEEP!"? As if having someone angrily scream that you should sleep is going to make it happen. It really is humorous how often we parents behave in ways, produced by our own reactivity, that consistently end up being counterproductive—we often work against our own goals!

A soothing response, in contrast, is not only more caring and compassionate, it's actually more effective. It will allow you to hold the line on your agreement with your son, but to do so in a way that acknowledges his feelings *and* helps him calm down so he can get to sleep. So you might say, "I can see how disappointed you are. You don't want to miss out. I know it's tough to have to go to bed when the

Instead of commanding and demanding...

And instead of just giving in...

Enforce boundaries, but soothe.

other boys are still up. That's hard, isn't it?" Then you could pause before saying, "Disappointment doesn't feel good, I know. Let me tuck you in, and we'll talk about a time you can have a friend over soon, and maybe even a sleepover of your own." That's a contingent response filled with compassion while honoring limits and structure.

You'll have to choose the words that feel right given who you are, and who your child is. Make sure to show empathy in your tone and nonverbal communication, and try not to lecture or use too many words. Just being present, pausing, and saying a few short empathic phrases is usually more effective than lecturing or overexplaining. The soothing moment can be handled in an infinite number of ways; the point is that *it's possible to hold the boundary even as you soothe.* Even though you're not giving in, you can still be there emotionally for your kids. Another way to say it is that you want to keep your relationship with your children on the front burner. Most other things, when it comes to behavior, can remain back-burner issues. Teach the lessons you need to teach, but do so in a way that values and prioritizes the relationship.

Keep your relationship with your children on the front burner. Most other things, when it comes to behavior, can remain back-burner issues. Teach the lessons you need to teach, but do so in a way that values and prioritizes the relationship.

What You Can Do: Strategies to Help Your Children Develop the Capacity to Self-soothe

As we said at the start of the chapter, one of our main goals for our kids when we offer a contingent response when they are hurting is that they'll develop the ability to have more autonomous inner self-soothing. When children are melting down, or sulking after losing a game, or experiencing anxiety about something at school, parents can offer the repeated experience of interactive soothing, where we work with them to reclaim calm and return to the green zone. Another way people might refer to this idea is "containing" or "holding the space," where we make it safe for our children to express strong or difficult emotions or thoughts, without reacting ourselves. As a result, they develop an internalized capacity to soothe themselves when they face obstacles and experience emotional distress. We soothe our children now, thus building their capacity to soothe themselves later when they need it and we're not around. What's more, they'll also be better at soothing others as friends, siblings (Yes, it really can happen!), partners, and eventually as parents themselves.

In addition to consistently showing up to soothe our kids when they need us, one of the best ways we can build the neurological circuits for inner self-soothing is to give them some specific tools they can use to create calm within themselves when inner chaos threatens to take over. Here are some strategies to help you do just that.

Strategy #1 to Promote Inner Self-soothing: Build a Calming Internal Toolkit

We mentioned above the idea of "proactive soothing," where rather than addressing emotional chaos only once it arrives in full form, you watch for ways to rein in the reactivity before it gets too intense. In this way, you can help your child from straying too far out of the green zone in the first place while also building the skills of emotional regulation and resilience. Building a calming toolkit is a similar idea, in that you look for ways to get ahead of a problem before it becomes difficult to manage. The basic idea is that you and your child work together *beforehand* to come up with some simple strategies to employ when he feels like he's going to move fully into either the red or blue zone.

First, chat with your child and explain the idea that, while disappointments and frus-

Teach kids that they can be problem solvers, thinking ahead and coming up with steps to take when they begin to feel their big emotions taking over.

trating situations will inevitably arise in life, we don't have to remain helpless in our response to them. We can be problem solvers, thinking ahead and coming up with steps to take when we begin to feel big emotions taking over.

The specific steps you and your child come up with are up to you, but here are a few suggestions.

CREATE A "CALM CAVE"

Sometimes we just need to get away, to remove ourselves from a high-stress situation. Our kids are no different. Having a place to retreat and recover when they feel strong emotions beginning to take over can be a great tool for returning to the green zone. So at a moment when your child feels calm and collected, take a few minutes to set up a "calm cave" she can go to the next time she becomes upset.

A small pup tent in the living room can serve this purpose, as can a corner of a closet, or a sheet over a desk or table. You and your child can fill the cave with favorite stuffed animals, a soft pillow and blanket, books, a pair of headphones, Play-Doh, or anything else that

The Calm Cave

gives your child comfort. Empower your child by letting her partici-
pate in the creation of the calming place. Then work to keep only
positive associations with the area. It won't stay a calming place if you
send your child there for punishment. But when your child is having
a hard time, you can offer it as a suggestion, almost as if it's a special
privilege: "Would you like to go to your quiet calm cave? It's okay
with me if you think that would help." Or, "What do you need right
now to help you feel better? Would you like for me to bring you a
snack in your special calming cave?" The point is to help her set up
an area where she feels relaxed and at ease, where she knows she can
go when she feels herself beginning to flip her lid.

CHOOSE SOME SOOTHING MUSIC

Another self-soothing tool to encourage your child to add to his
calming toolkit is a song he can sing or listen to when he becomes
upset. The song will be different for different children. Your child
might find classical music calming. Another might like Motown or
the intricate and joyful music of Dan's son, Alex Siegel. (Excuse the
plug of a proud dad here!) Some kids respond well to forest or beach

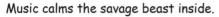
Music calms the savage beast inside.

sounds or guided visualizations. Or if your child is more eclectic, you might even create a playlist he can turn to when he needs help calming himself down. That way he can click through various songs and styles and find one that helps quell the chaos he's experiencing. Even the act of putting in the earbuds and choosing a song can help him take a proactive step to help himself.

COME UP WITH A LIST OF ENERGY-RELEASING MOVEMENTS

In addition to having a cave to escape to and some music to play, one of the best and simplest self-soothing tricks to teach kids is simply to move their bodies. Dancing, running in place, swinging, dribbling a ball, twirling around—anything that moves the body has the potential to decrease nervous-system arousal. Bodily movement has a direct effect on brain activity. In fact, the body is sending the brain information all the time, including regarding emotions. You know this from times your stomach hurt when you felt anxious, or your

teeth clenched when you were angry, or your shoulders tensed when you were on high alert. That's the body sending messages, whether we're consciously aware of those emotions or not.

A person's emotional state can completely change when the body moves vigorously. Anger, frustration, tension, and other negative emotions are released so that emotional balance can return. To put it differently, movement soothes the body and the emotions it experiences.

> A person's emotional state can completely change when the body moves vigorously. Anger, frustration, tension, and other negative emotions are released so that emotional balance can return.

This is a simple concept to teach to even the youngest children. We know one mom who, after hearing us speak, began implementing this practice on a regular basis. She said she'll first acknowledge her kids' feelings and let them feel her empathy—this is key—then immediately get them moving. She might have them run around the house, or she'll say something like, "Run with me to the backyard. I think I hear that bird we were looking at yesterday." Whatever it takes to get them using their muscles and moving their bodies. Her children are young, three and five, and she told us, "As the kids get older I'm sure I'll have to change my strategies on this, but at the moment, getting them to move breaks through the hurt feelings better than just about anything we do."

Like any other technique, this one won't work every time. It's just one tool in your kit. But it's a consistently effective way to help alter a child's emotional state. And if you can help your child understand what you're doing, she'll have one more strategy to use herself when she needs it. By the time she's a teenager, she might even realize, when she's upset, that one of the best things she can do is to go for a run.

COME UP WITH A "DISTRESS SIGNAL"

The final tool we'll mention here is to teach kids that they don't *always* have to use internal self-soothing strategies. They're not on their own. In fact, one of the best ways they can help themselves—young and old kids alike (and even adults)—is to ask for help when they need it. Throughout our life we may need others to help us regulate our own inner state. This co-regulation is found in close relationships no matter our age. Young children especially need this early in life, but we all need to balance our inner resources for regulation with the interregulation that comes from our contingent connections with other people.

There are times when we need someone else to step in and lend a hand. Maybe we just need to talk. Or cry. Or be hugged. As we've said, this is especially the case for our children when they're young. They need us to be there and show them what soothing looks like. But even as they grow and develop, there will be plenty of times they can't quite get on top of whatever it is that has them down. So an important ability to cultivate is to recognize when we need to ask for help.

Talk to your kids about paying attention to what's going on inside them, and explain the importance of asking for help when they need

it. This is how you focus on both the inner and the inter aspects of soothing. You might have a child who is especially adept at expressing himself in such situations. But many kids aren't. In that case create with them a "distress signal," possibly a code word they can use that means, "I need help. I don't know how to calm myself down right now." Maybe it's a word they think sounds funny, like "boysenberry," or a made-up silly term, or they might choose a more common term like "cardboard." Or you might not even use words and instead decide on a nonverbal code, so that when they tug at their earlobe, they're telling you, "I need help here."

It doesn't really matter how they send the message. The key is that they understand that, even as they're learning to internally self-soothe, there are going to be times they still need you to show up and lend a hand for their interactive self-soothing.

The most obvious reward your children reap when you work with them to help them learn to soothe themselves internally and interactively is that when they face difficult and painful situations as they enter adolescence and adulthood, they'll be better at dealing with those moments on their own, learning the resourceful skills of both internal and interactive regulation. Another related and significant benefit is that by providing them with a calming toolbox full of various tactics for dealing with their emotional pain, you empower them. They understand that they have at their disposal specific strategies they can use when they feel themselves going out of control. Some strategies will be internal, some interactive. We need both across our lives. If red-zone anger is threatening to take over, or a blue-zone cloud has overcome them and all they want to do is shut down and hide, they have specific steps they can take so they're no longer at the mercy of their feelings and circumstances.

Notice, too, that as with most whole-brain principles and strategies, everything here applies to adults as well. (So maybe you want to go clear out some room in the back of your own closet for a stash of chocolate?)

Strategy #2 to Promote Inner Self-soothing: Offer Your P-E-A-C-E

There are all kinds of techniques we can use and strategies we can try when our kids are upset. We've listed a few here, and countless others appear in parenting books and online resources, as well as in your own creative mind. But the fact is that there's no magic bullet that will work every time, no "one right answer" for what to say or do to help your kids feel better when they're hurting.

Presence

Engagement

Affection

Calm

Empathy

There is, though, an overall response to your children's pain that will virtually always be correct. It may not always be effective in terms of helping your kids calm down, and it might not always immediately produce the results you desire. But in terms of showing up for your kids and demonstrating what love and soothing look like, it's the right thing to do. You can offer your kids your P-E-A-C-E: your presence, engagement, affection, calm, and empathy.

Let's discuss what P-E-A-C-E means, specifically. Each letter of the acronym represents a key component of what it means to show up for your children when they are dealing with some form of emotional distress.

PRESENCE

When your kids are hurting, be there for them. Show up, and do so with presence. We've discussed this concept throughout the book, and it's never more important than when our children are suffering in some way and need our help. Presence means an open state of awareness, a receptive way of being that invites connection. In this mindset, we don't judge our kids but instead see them, as clearly as

When your child needs you, be there.

The Many Ways We
Communicate Nonverbally

Facial Expressions

Eye Contact

Tone of Voice

Posture

Gestures

Timing of Response

Intensity

we can, for who they actually are. We make ourselves available to them, open and receptive to them, and they know that they are our priority and that they're not alone.

Sometimes your child might have to wait until you get home from work, or if you're on a business trip, he might have to talk to you on the phone. But he knows that when he needs you, you'll be there.

Keep in mind, presence is also about being attuned enough to your child, and to the situation, that you can recognize moments when he *doesn't* want you to be with him, physically. You might determine that the best thing you can say is, "I'm going to give you some space now. I'll be in the kitchen if you need me." The point, then, is that your presence is offered and available. Your child won't ever wonder whether you care, or whether you'll be there when he needs you.

ENGAGEMENT

The second part of P-E-A-C-E is about truly engaging when you show up. The idea here is *the way* you offer your presence. You actively listen. You use your nonverbal communication to express how important your child is, and how much you value and care about what she's telling you. You make eye contact. You nod your head. You put your arm around her, or hold her while she cries. You offer your presence, and you offer it in a way that fully engages with your child and her pain, not talking her out of it, not minimizing it, not lecturing.

Here's an exercise to help you think about different ways to connect using nonverbal communication. Using your hands, working from the top down, point out each of seven nonverbal signals to remind yourself of the many ways you can engage with your child without ever saying a word. Start by taking your index finger and circling it around your face, representing facial expressions. Then point to your eyes, which stand for eye contact. Now, point to your throat, which represents tone of voice. Now point to your shoulders and body, which denote your posture. Move your hands and arms, which stand for gestures. Point to your wrist (where a watch would be) for the timing of your response, and finally, make fists with your hands, showing the energy or intensity of your response.

When it's time to engage with our child to help soothe her, we can take a virtually infinite number of approaches. Find the one that works best for you.

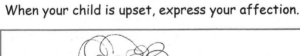

When your child is upset, express your affection.

AFFECTION

Part of fully engaging is finding both explicit and implicit ways to express your affection. You communicate, with both your words and your actions, how much love you feel for your child. How much compassion about what he's going through. How much you desire to help if you can. One of the most powerful ways to soothe someone—child or adult—is to help that person feel fully, absolutely loved.

CALM

Remaining calm is sometimes one of the most difficult parts of offering your P-E-A-C-E. In certain situations it won't present much of a challenge—say if your child is upset about playground politics that have nothing directly to do with you. But if she has just failed a test she assured you she was prepared for, or some other conflict that results in an attack on you, then remaining calm within yourself may prove to be a real challenge. In that situation, it's all the more important that *you* remain in the green zone yourself. You need to be the adult in the relationship. You can be upset, of course; there's nothing wrong with experiencing whatever you feel at that moment and, at

In the midst of conflict, create calm.

the right time, expressing your emotions in an appropriate manner. But the more you can model for your child how to say what you feel without going on the attack or losing control, the more she will learn about both emotional management and relational respect.

One of our favorite techniques to help bring calm to a situation when a child is upset is to get below the child's eye level during the discussion. Doing so communicates, to both of you, that you have no intention of being a threat of any kind. Remember that if "threat" is communicated in any way to your child, your child's brain may go into threat-response mode. When you position your body in a way that's the opposite of threat, by sitting in a relaxed posture below their eye level, you communicate "no threat." Your child will recognize that she doesn't have to remain in a defensive posture, that she doesn't have to fight, and that she can lay down her figurative sword and shield.

In getting below eye level, you're not taking a submissive position. That's not what this is about, and you can and should remain the parent in the situation. It's simply a strategic posture to interactively down-regulate your child's nervous system. It's like you're turning down the intense reactivity. Sometimes it can even help to imagine slowly turning down a volume dial. You're simply communicating, through your posture and body language, that rather than being a threat, you're available to your child even though you are upset with each other. This works because when we use nonthreatening body language, it activates a totally different neural network than if we're in an aggressive, imposing posture. The brain gets the message from the body that it's safe and that there's no need to fight.

EMPATHY

The final aspect of offering your P-E-A-C-E is empathy, which means that even when you haven't personally experienced what another person is dealing with, you're sensitive to that experience to the extent that you can *feel with them*. Empathy has other components as

In the midst of pain, show empathy.

well, such as perspective taking, cognitive understanding, empathic joy, and empathic concern. In a caring, securely attached parent-child relationship, empathy springs from parental attunement and allows the child to *feel felt*. Especially when combined with presence, engagement, affection, and calm, empathy can help create an optimal environment for getting your child on the road back to the green zone.

Again, there's no formula that will cure all emotional ills or fix every problem your child faces. But when you can offer your P-E-A-C-E, you'll ensure that your child will feel attuned to, cared for, and loved—all of which are significant steps toward soothing.

Showing Up for Ourselves

Life is beautiful, full of wonder and meaning. *And* it's also painful and extremely difficult at times. Each of us, without exception, has to face obstacles and difficulties and setbacks and heartbreak. We're challenged by moments that require every ounce of our strength and courage. Treasured relationships end. We face a devastating loss.

We're shaken by difficult changes in our health, our career, our family, our finances, or some other crucial life situation.

If we're fortunate, we have attachment figures in our adult life, key individuals within our support system of family, partners, and/or friends to help us through the most challenging times. And some of us received secure attachment from our caregivers when we were young, providing us with the integrated neural circuitry that gives us the strength and resilience to weather storms. We felt safe, seen, and soothed by someone while our brains were developing, and now we have a secure inner model of attachment so that when life's inevitable hardships appear, we know we can get through them, even if it means merely enduring and surviving the present moment.

Again, though, that's if we're fortunate. Plenty of us—somewhere around four out of ten—were *not* nurtured like that when we were young. We *didn't* have the type of family that kept us safe, or that made us feel seen. Some of us had inconsistent attachment experiences, so we didn't develop an internal means of soothing ourselves, and instead relied even more on unreliable others. In this situation of ambivalent attachment, we developed the strategy of increased drive for connection. Others of us, instead, had the experience of avoidant attachment with our primary caregivers. In this case we had to develop some kind of internal mechanism, a mental model, to decrease our drive for connection, literally disconnecting from not only our own internal worlds, but also from the relational connections with others. What's more, with avoidant attachment, when we were hurting, we were all alone. No one was there to soothe us when we were angry, or disappointed, or injured, or in any other kind of distress. We had to handle life's challenges by ourselves.

When we were hurting, we were all alone. No one was there to soothe us when we were angry, or disappointed, or injured, or in any other kind of distress. We had to handle life's challenges by ourselves.

And in the case of disorganized attachment, our caregiver was a source of terror, and we had the internal experience of a drive toward the caregiver for protection but, at the same time, a drive away from that person—the source of distress. That fragmenting experience can lead to an internal state of dissociation, especially under stress. Even our sense of reality, our epistemic trust, can be on shaky ground when such a biological paradox is our attachment legacy. Both internal and interactive means of soothing are compromised, and even our sense of what can be trusted as real can be fragmented in the experience of disorganized attachment.

Think for a moment about your own experiences, specifically as they relate to how soothed you felt when you were upset in some way. Was your internal landscape attended to? Look at the following questions, giving yourself a few moments with each, as you consider your own experiences, both past and present. The more clear you can get on your own past, the more benefits you'll reap in terms of self-knowledge as well as in your relationship with your children.

1. When you experienced distress as a child, who was there for you? What specific memories do you have of a parent or caregiver showing up and providing you with their P-E-A-C-E?

2. If you did receive this type of attunement when you were upset, what aspects of it would you want to give to your own kids?

3. If this kind of nurturing was missing from your childhood experience, how did you learn to cope with that absence? Did you most often simply remain upset until you just cried it out? Did you learn to deny your feelings and ignore their importance?

4. How do you handle your own difficult moments now, as an adult? Do you have someone who supports you as you deal with challenging experiences? Do you have a difficult time returning to the green zone once you've left it? When you're angry, upset, or disappointed, are you more likely to experience a red-zone emotional flood (where your emotions take over) or a blue-zone emotional desert (where you shut down and ignore what's going on inside you)?

5. How present are you for your kids when they're hurting? Do you provide them with your P-E-A-C-E? Can they count on your being there with your presence, your engagement, your affection, your calm, your empathy? Or are they sometimes left to deal with their difficulties alone?

6. Are there times you get so caught up in your kids' emotions that you amplify their distress? In other words, are you co-escalating, instead of co-regulating?

7. Take a moment and think specifically about each of your kids, individually. For each child, get a mental image of what he or she looks like when they're upset in some way. You know them well enough to know the most likely reason. Maybe you have an especially sensitive child who becomes easily overwhelmed. Or maybe an older child is currently upset about a boundary you've set regarding screen time or bedtime. Whoever your kids are, think about what they'll be feeling and thinking when things don't go their way. How do you want to respond? Considering your own experiences as a child, how can you most effectively offer your P-E-A-C-E to your own children? Do you want to do better at being present? At fully engaging? At being more affectionate, calm, or empathic? Even if you didn't receive from your own parents the kind of soothing you needed, you can show up and provide it for your kids. How do you want to make that happen the next time they need you?

Showing up for your kids is about being there for them, even, and maybe especially, when they're at their worst. That's when they need you the most. So spend the time in your own inner reflections developing a more coherent narrative about the way you yourself were parented. You can learn new and helpful strategies—both inner and inter—for soothing your own inner states of distress. In constructing a clear understanding of who you are now and the emerging coherent narrative of how relationships have shaped you, you can earn and learn security in your life. In addition, by learning new and helpful techniques of inner and inter soothing, within yourself and in connecting with others, you'll gain not only a clarity of understanding but also your own emotional state of calm. As a result you'll be able to provide your kids with P-E-A-C-E; they'll grow into adolescents and adults who know what it feels like to be nurtured and soothed; and they'll learn how to provide that kind of care for themselves and for those they love.

$\underline{S}$ecure

CHAPTER 6

Putting All the S's Together
Helping Your Kids Feel SECURE

Now we come to the final S and focus on what this whole book has been building toward: creating a sense of security in your children. When kids feel safe, seen, and soothed, they come to feel secure as they become securely attached.

To illustrate, let us tell you about a conflict one father, Jamal, had with his twelve-year-old son, Clay. Clay's scouting group had returned from a week-long camping trip, and to celebrate their accomplishment, the group was going to see a movie together. The boys selected a movie that was rated R, and when Jamal read about it online, it was clear to him that it was not an appropriate film for his twelve-year-old son. A couple of other parents expressed some misgivings when Jamal asked them about the decision, but they all responded with some form of, "I don't love it either, but all the other boys are going, so . . ." Jamal also hated giving Clay the news that he was going to miss out on the fun experience with his buddies, but he felt no ambiguity when it came to his conclusion. Clay couldn't go.

As expected, Clay was furious. He first expressed his shock as he entered the red zone of chaos: "Are you serious?! But *everyone's* going!" Then he began to lash out at his father, yelling, "Do you even remember what it was like to be a kid? I'm the only one not going! I can't believe you want me to be left out!" Jamal tried to explain, even offering to take him to a different movie at the same time in the same theater so he could be with his friends before and after, but, understandably, Clay wasn't interested in this "stupid" alternative solution and attacked his dad again: "You don't even care enough to try to understand." With that he literally turned his back on his dad and went to his room, a slammed door his last word on the subject.

Moments like this are tough. We don't want our children to miss out, but sometimes, in order to offer the first S and keep them safe, we have to tell them no. And even though Jamal knew he was making the right decision—he knew Clay wasn't ready for the images and ideas in the movie—he still didn't like knowing that his son would feel deprived of this important bonding experience with his friends, and that he was so angry with his father.

After a few minutes Clay reappeared, apparently wanting to dish out some more. He alternated between pleading his case one moment and castigating his father the next. Jamal held his ground in terms of his decision—he saw no wiggle room there—but he kept his focus on his priorities: protecting his son while keeping their relationship as the front-burner issue. He repeatedly avoided taking the bait and escalating the situation by resorting to the same reactivity Clay was displaying—even when things got a bit personal and Clay told his father that he couldn't understand because he'd never even had any friends when he was a kid.

Remaining calm in the face of this kind of onslaught can be a Herculean feat. How did Jamal do that? By focusing on the other S's. He prioritized *seeing* his son and understanding where the anger was coming from. It made perfect sense that Clay would feel angry, and Jamal told him so. ("I know, dude. It can feel awful, and even embarrassing, to be the odd man out.") He also approached the situation with curiosity rather than reactivity and let himself feel compassion, even as Clay momentarily lashed out. In doing so, he offered a *soothing* presence. He didn't lower himself to the rhetorical level his son had chosen and attack back, saying, "I'm the dad and I didn't ask for your opinion. This is not a democracy!" And he didn't shut the whole thing down with the old threat approach: "Watch yourself, young man. If you keep this up you won't be seeing your friends for a long time." These kinds of parental comebacks are incredibly tempting because we start to feel attacked and reactive, but there's no way Clay could have felt soothed or calmer if his dad had gone in that direction. His nervous system would have remained in a heightened state of arousal, and the relationship would have suffered the consequences. It would have been a lose-lose situation.

Instead, Jamal remained the adult—a mature, regulated adult—in the situation and allowed Clay to express himself. Jamal focused on providing his P-E-A-C-E (presence, engagement, affection, calm, and empathy), saying things like, "I know you're disappointed" and "I don't blame you for being mad."

He had already taught Clay through the years about boundaries. He knew his son was momentarily being disrespectful and lashing out from a place of reactivity, and that this wasn't his typical way of talking to his dad. In offering P-E-A-C-E along with giving Clay time to deal with and move through his big emotions, he soothed him back into the green zone.

What was Jamal doing for his son throughout the entire interaction, beginning with the decision not to allow him to see the movie, all the way through the eventual respite from the outburst? He was providing the first three S's. Clay was safe, seen, and ultimately soothed. And in providing the first three, Jamal was thereby providing his son with the fourth and ultimate S: security. Even in the midst of his anger

Even in the midst of his anger and resentment, Clay was learning about his father, who was modeling for him the way parents provide secure attachment: They keep their kids safe even when it means making an unpopular decision; they see and listen even when a child is lashing out; and they make efforts to soothe and offer P-E-A-C-E when their children are upset.

Instead of reacting...

Offer your P-E-A-C-E.

and resentment, Clay was learning about his father, who was modeling for him the way parents provide secure attachment: They keep
their kids safe even when it means making an unpopular decision;
they see and listen even when a child is lashing out (while drawing
boundaries at times regarding respectful communication); and they

make efforts to soothe and offer P-E-A-C-E when their children are upset.

And once Clay calmed down, these lessons could be internalized and added to all the other moments when Jamal showed him what it means to love someone and show up for them. As a result, Clay continued developing a secure attachment with his father, along with the strength and resilience to go through life with a sense of inner strength and an understanding of the power of relationships.

One of the wonderful things about this dynamic—providing security for our kids—is that over time, they will actually depend on us *less* for it. Relationships will always be important—even secure individuals rely on others and find meaning and significance in connection—but as kids grow up, having security makes it less and less *necessary* that someone else provide the other S's in every situation. Their security will become established as an overall mental model of their identity, and they'll have the internal resources to keep *themselves* safe, to see *themselves* as worthy, to soothe *themselves* when things go wrong.

As kids grow up, having security makes it less and less *necessary* that someone else provide the other S's in every situation. Their security will become established as an overall mental model of their identity, and they'll have the internal resources to keep *themselves* safe, to see *themselves* as worthy, to soothe *themselves* when things go wrong.

Put differently, there's an *internal working model* of security that's created within the mind of a child when she feels safe, seen, and soothed on a relatively predictable and consistent basis (and when repair is made when that consistency isn't always present). "Working" means it is open to change, and also that it is our mental model that works on many levels of our mind's functioning. This working model directly shapes how we see ourselves in the world, how we learn to regulate our own emotional state, and how we engage with others in our lives. In many ways, our internal working model of attachment is what shapes our relationships, which in turn helps shape who we ourselves are. As a result, a child develops a schema—a generalization based on repeated experiences—that says, "My inner life is worthy of being seen." Not entitled, just a sense of inner worth that says, "My inner world—my feelings, my thoughts, my dreams, my longings, my meaning of things, the story of who I am—these are good and worthy of being shared with others." That's security. That's the internal working model Jamal was building in his son Clay in moments like the one described above.

Let's look at another example. One scenario we see from time to time involves a child who presents behavioral challenges—not necessarily when she's upset, but as a way of testing boundaries. Perhaps it's a three-year-old who consistently hits her baby brother, but again, not in the middle of a tantrum, but seemingly *just because*. From time to time parents ask us how to respond in a situation like this. We say to these parents that, again, every child is different, and while there's no one-size-fits-all disciplinary approach, the Four S's are almost always what the situation calls for.

For instance, if you were the parent in this situation, you'd provide safety, protecting the baby brother, just as you would for the big sister. You'd also work hard to really see your three-year-old. It might seem as if she's just acting out at random, and that she's not really upset about anything in particular. But on closer inspection, when you "chased the why" and approached the situation with curiosity, you'd likely determine that she was seeking your attention, probably because the baby was claiming so much of it. Then, having seen her need—whether for your attention or something else—you could acknowledge and respond based on what you observed, all while setting clear boundaries.

And finally you would soothe your young daughter. You might tell her, "Everyone will be safe in our family. I won't let you hurt your brother, so I'm going to help you calm down. We can go to your peaceful place, or I can hold you right here."

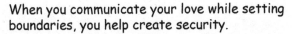

When you communicate your love while setting boundaries, you help create security.

You'd be helping her understand that when she has big emotions, or she feels the need to test limits and doesn't handle herself well, she can still feel secure in your love. You'd soothe whatever it was that was raging within her, whatever was driving her to hit her brother, all while keeping both children safe. And she'd learn that you'll consistently show up to see her needs and respond to them in a timely, sensitive, predictable manner. As a result she would develop the security that serves her for a lifetime.

Simply put, children with secure attachment—those who have been fortunate enough to acquire a secure internal working model of attachment—develop the characteristics and skills that allow them to live happier and more successful lives. The benefits of security (see page 202) are striking.

These characteristics of securely attached children are what they carry with them, even when parents and other attachment figures aren't physically present. From a neuroplasticity perspective, the repeated experiences that lead to security change the brain and produce within children intra- and interpersonal skills and attributes

the Benefits of SECURITY:

→ An understanding of the importance of relationships

→ Independence and objectivity, even in the context of connection with others

→ Resilience in the face of stress

→ Regulation of emotions and body

→ Freedom to reflect on the past, and integrate it with the present as adaptable plans are made for the future

→ An ability to provide attuned communication

→ Flexibility and adaptability

→ Empathy

→ Personal insight and the capacity to develop a rich inner life

that allow them to find more joy, meaning, and significance in their lives. This is what a secure working model of attachment creates.

When kids don't enjoy this type of security with an attachment figure, the opposite typically applies. Their relational capacity often decreases, as do resilience, adaptability, self-reliance, and the other characteristics. Think back to the descriptions of the various forms of insecure attachment. Sometimes a child will develop an avoidant attachment pattern, where she learns to ignore her own emotions and avoids communicating her needs. Doing so would obviously make relationships much more difficult and decrease her personal insight, leaving her less aware of her inner world, and less apt to request help when she needs it. Likewise, a child who develops an ambivalent attachment pattern and feels like he can't count on people to be predictable may miss out on several of the attributes listed. He might have trouble calming his own emotions, or he may lack the ability or inclination to openly share himself with others out of fear that they won't show up for him in turn. And kids with a disorganized attachment pattern will likely have the most difficulty of all when it comes to enjoying the benefits of secure attachment. If they are led to believe, based on their interactions with a caregiver, that people are dangerous and unreliable, then that perspective may ruthlessly im-

When you provide a child with security...

She develops the capacity to provide it for herself.

pose itself on their lives, preventing them from experiencing many of the advantages that children with secure attachment get to enjoy.

Security, on the other hand, brings with it a sense of empowerment. In terms of safety, a child with secure attachment believes that she can protect herself, that she's worthy of protection, and that she can seek out safety when she needs it. She fully expects safety to be an inherent quality in her life. Likewise, she can see and soothe herself. She learns that if she's in a state of distress, she has skills that enable her to monitor what's going on within her, and then to soothe and regulate her own inner life.

As she grows up she'll carry this security with her, interacting with the world from an inner sense of well-being, an internal sense of coherence and resilience. She'll feel worthy and able to connect with others, and understand the different forces within herself. As a result of having at least one person show up for her in a consistent way, she'll live her life and make her decisions from what we call a secure base, which will create feelings of both safety and courage.

> As a result of having at least one person show up for her in a consistent way, she'll live her life and make her decisions from what we call a secure base, which will create feelings of both safety and courage.

Secure Base: Safe Haven and Launching Pad

It's easy to see why having at least one caregiver who reliably and consistently (if not perfectly) shows up to meet their needs and pay attention to their inner realities helps children develop a secure base from which they can explore the world. Then, from this base, they can venture beyond what they already know, surveying their landscape and investigating the world around them. That's the goal. When kids don't feel reliably safe, seen, and soothed, the opposite is the case: There's no security. Children without caregivers who show up to provide the Four S's often demonstrate challenges with close relationships, difficulty reasoning under stressful conditions, or anxiety about trying new things or leaving their comfort zone. That's why it's so important that we help kids develop a secure attachment.

Children without caregivers who show up to provide the Four S's often demonstrate challenges with close relationships, difficulty reasoning under stressful conditions, or anxiety about trying new things or leaving their comfort zone.

Think about a toddler with a shy temperament who visits a playground for the first time. In a secure attachment model, he might hold on to his father's leg when first set down at the bench near the jungle gym. Then he might take a few steps toward the play structure, until a bigger child runs by and frightens him. At this point he hurries back to his dad, then ventures out again, this time getting closer to the slide. As soon as he thinks about how far he is from his father, he might return to him, his secure base. Then he might try again, actually reaching the ladder he's interested in. These progressive expeditions into parts unknown both challenge the child and strengthen him. And he's willing to confront his fear and increase the distance between himself and his father precisely because he has faith that his father will be there for him when he returns. He counts on there being a secure base any time he needs it, so he feels okay undertaking bigger and bigger risks along the way. The safety provided by the secure base allows him to take on more and more.

As a child learns from these repeated and reliable experiences of connection, his brain changes its structure and grows in more integrative ways, enabling more effective regulation. What was an external set of interactions of connection with his father now becomes an internal set of connections in his brain. Then, when a challenge arises, this now-internalized secure model serves as the source of personal resilience. The child can now face difficulties in an open manner, and when things get tough and don't turn out as expected, he can get back up and try again. That's the resilient mind of a securely attached child.

A helpful explanation of this process comes from Circle of Security International (COS), an organization that has strengthened families all over the world by teaching parents about the importance of attachment, and how having a parent who consistently shows up can enlarge a child's circle of security. As explained in the COS book *The Circle of Security Intervention,* a child's circle widens when her parent offers two foundational "spaces": a launching pad and a safe harbor. The circle of security involves supporting a child's exploration by offering her a launching pad from which she can take off, while also remaining a haven of safety, a place she can return to in a storm.

The circle of security involves supporting a child's exploration by offering her a launching pad from which she can take off, while also remaining a haven of safety, a place she can return to in a storm.

We nurture with the safe harbor, and we support and encourage with the launching pad.

As the child with a secure base grows older, this process will repeat itself in different facets of his life. His first day of preschool might be terrifying, and he might need his father to stay with him for a while before joining the other kids on the rug. The next day, though, he might require his father to stay for a shorter time. He feels confident letting go more quickly each subsequent day because he's learned, via repeated experiences throughout his young life, that his dad is going to show up for him over and over again. With each expedition outward as he grows up—learning to ride a bike, joining a sports team, performing a song at his piano recital, attending sleep-away camp, on up through eventually leaving for college—this temperamentally reserved child develops confidence, resilience, and a belief that he can face difficult and scary obstacles. His circle of security continues to strengthen, helping him feel safe in the world. He knows that he can always come home. And he will. He has the two components of a secure base—a reliable and nurturing safe harbor, and a supportive, encouraging launching pad.

A Secure Base Produces Strength, Not a Sense of Entitlement

Don't worry. Offering your kids unconditional emotional support and a secure base is not going to make them soft, or spoiled, or fragile. And it's not going to create feelings of entitlement. We get some form of that question from time to time, where a parent will say, "The world is a tough place, and it's my job to toughen them up. I don't want to coddle them."

> Offering your kids unconditional emotional support is not going to make them soft. They will explore more courageously, and venture farther out, than children who haven't received that kind of attention and care.

We understand the fear behind the concern, but let us put your mind at ease. Kids whose emotional needs are quickly, sensitively, and consistently met will *not* fall apart if someone isn't there for them all the time. If you let your frightened five-year-old sleep in your bed sometimes, that doesn't mean he'll need to be there for the rest of his life.

In fact, the research shows just the opposite. Kids who believe that their caregivers will show up for them over and over again develop the independence and resilience that give them the self-

Meeting a child's emotional needs...

Does NOT produce a spoiled or entitled adult.

confidence to step beyond their comfort zones. They will explore more courageously, and venture farther out, than children who haven't received that kind of attention and care.

Yes, there may come a time, for whatever reason, that you decide not to allow your kids to sleep in your bed. But don't make that decision out of a fear that meeting their emotional needs will somehow harm them. Spoiling a child means giving in to her every whim, or buying her every object she ever desires. But paying attention to her emotional needs? That's not spoiling her. That's not coddling. It's called attuning or connecting. And that's what makes her feel secure enough to go out and explore on her own as she grows. It doesn't make her entitled and fragile; it makes her resilient. The research shows that when a child feels safe enough, she will venture to independence as she is developmentally ready, and that pushing her to that stage when she's not ready—where she experiences the opposite of safety—can backfire, actually causing greater dependence.

Research shows that when a child feels safe enough, she will venture to independence as she is developmentally ready, and that pushing her to that stage when she's not ready—where she experiences the opposite of safety—can backfire, actually causing greater dependence.

A related objection we hear when we discuss the importance of emotional consistency from parents has to do with earning a child's respect. One parent will often tell us that her spouse objects to the strategy of connecting with a child before addressing behavioral issues. He might say, "They're never going to respect you when you let them walk all over you like that. You need to be harsh sometimes. At times you even need to yell." And she fears he's right.

Our position, based on science and experience, is that parents can maintain authority while prioritizing the relationship and maintaining self-control.

We do agree with this father that parents shouldn't allow kids to "walk all over them." It is indeed important that parents remain the authorities in the relationship—you've heard us say so throughout the book. But our position, based on science and experience, is that parents can maintain authority while prioritizing the relationship and maintaining self-control.

When parents are yelling and reactive, commanding and demanding, having lost control of themselves, how does that earn respect from a child? It's much more likely to come when you stay in charge of your emotions, when you remain thoughtful, measured, calm, and fair-minded. That's strength, not weakness. It's like the Little League coach who keeps his cool with his players, versus the one who's always flying off the handle, yelling at the kids and umpires. The latter might create fear, even order on his team. But it will come at a cost. And respect? Not as likely. All things being equal, the kids will respect (and even like) the coach who can be strong and smart from a position of knowing who he is and how he wants to interact with kids and other adults, and who maintains strong relationships.

Plus, when your go-to response when your kids do something you don't like is to scream to enforce your point—especially if it appears that you've lost it—there can be consequences to the relationship. Maybe you actually get compliance and fewer "conduct problems" in the short term. But as with the coach, at what cost? Rather than engendering "respect" from your children, it can change, in negative ways, how they feel about you, and whether they'll come to you when they want to share something.

Let us remind you, by the way, that we're not saying you're doing irreparable harm if you raise your voice with your kids sometimes. Expressing your emotions is fine, and sometimes that comes with volume and intensity. Our point is simply that authority is *not* inherently linked to force or severity. You can maintain your kids' respect and remain the authority in the house even when you never raise your voice. And again, as always, remember that when you do flip your lid or handle things in ways that don't feel good to you or your child, it's important to apologize and repair the breach in the relationship as quickly as you can.

To sum up this point, there are definitely times when we allow our kids to face challenges and overcome obstacles, even when doing so is difficult. For them to develop strength and resilience, we have to set boundaries and tell them no. But we need to be discerning as we decide how much struggle they can endure, and we always—yes,

Respect comes not from severity and yelling...

But from being strong and smart, knowing who you are and how you want to interact with those around you.

always—want to provide emotional support along the way. If we mess up, we can always make a repair with a sincere apology. And we can try to learn from such ruptures in a way that results in growth and a stronger relationship with our kids. We'll be offering them a role model of how to be human and create connection. In doing so we provide both the safe haven and the launching pad they can depend on as they develop the strength and independence that allow them to live their lives with purpose and meaning.

Positive, Tolerable, and Toxic Stress

One factor to consider in thinking about how to help our kids feel secure when they face challenges is the type of stress the situation presents. Did you know that not all stress is bad for you? In fact, researchers talk about a phenomenon called *positive* stress, which occurs when we feel pressure to perform in a way that motivates us without overwhelming or engulfing us. It might make us study hard for a test, or be more productive, or perform well under pressure. Positive stress can mobilize and even invigorate us, nudging us to accomplish tasks we might not otherwise be able to.

More challenging is what's called *tolerable* stress, which is pressure that we can endure, but that isn't inherently beneficial. It can be positive and helpful or it can be negative and harmful, depending on the context. For example, leaving the secure base we've provided may feel stressful to children. Remember the toddler trepidatiously making his way across the foreign playground. When his father provides the safe haven to which he can return, then that stress remains relatively manageable. In fact, it can even become a positive force, in that as he reaches his goal of the jungle gym, he has conquered not only the distance between his father and the slide, but his own fears as well. He has undergone what we see as a minor amount of stress—even though it didn't feel minor to him at the time—and come out okay on the other side. The stress he experienced has actually acted in his favor.

Notice, though, that the toddler could endure this stress because someone provided enough support to make it tolerable. In fact, that's an essential part of tolerable stress: Whether it has a beneficial or adverse effect depends largely on whether the person receives the support to handle it, and on how long the individual must tolerate the pressure.

Security Makes Stress More Tolerable

Positive Stress

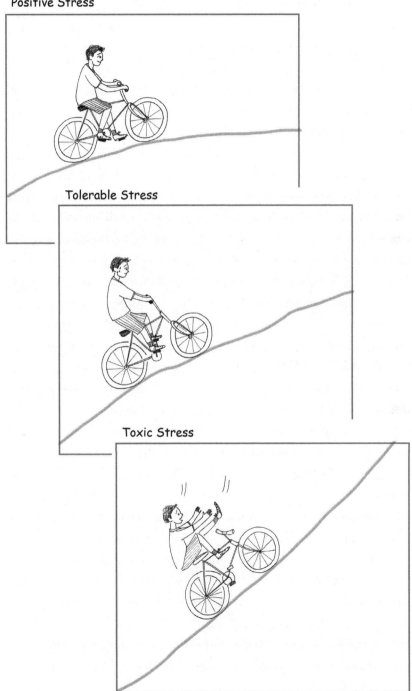

Tolerable Stress

Toxic Stress

When a person is asked to face more than he can handle, or to do so alone, or to do so for too long, it produces what's called *toxic* stress, which can become harmful. It has the potential to take a significant toll on development, on the life trajectory and quality of life, even including physical health and life expectancy. This is the kind of stress that results from the adverse childhood experiences (ACEs) we discussed previously. Especially in the life of a child, toxic stress contains the potential for trauma that can produce long-lasting harm.

Again, one of the key factors in determining whether a particular event causes stress that is positive, tolerable, or toxic is whether the person experiencing the stress has sufficient support. Without secure attachment, a stressor that might have been relatively manageable can move into the toxic category if a child is left to handle the adversity alone or hasn't developed the secure working model that offers an internal resource of resilience. With secure attachment, though, some stressors that might be damaging to someone without it can become not only tolerable but even positive, perhaps promoting resilience. Recall the slope metaphor from the first chapter, where we talked about a child bicycling up a hill. The more security we provide for our kids, the more the difficulties they experience will produce tolerable or positive stress, as opposed to toxic stress.

Granted, sometimes life will deal us the toxic-stress card. Even securely attached children with parents who consistently show up will at times be forced to deal with a situation no child should ever have to face. A secure base won't protect them from all the harsh realities of life—it's not a guarantee of a life without challenges. But the Four S's can serve as a protective buffer. They can help a child transform adversity into resilience and growth. Whereas feeling unsafe leads to toxicity, safety makes trouble tolerable. Feeling seen can do the same. And being soothed can diminish the physiological toll of nervous system hyperarousal and the chaos that threatens to take over; it helps regulate a person so that the stress remains tolerable. To put it differently, the Four F reactions (fight, flight, freeze, faint) aren't called upon as frequently because the Four S's show up and do their job. That's what the resilience of secure attachment is all about.

What You Can Do: Strategies That Promote a Secure Base for Your Child

Strategy #1 for Promoting a Secure Base: Invest in a Relational Trust Fund

When you show up for your kids, you build trust with them. Each time they need you and you're there for them, the trust in the relationship goes up. It's like making a deposit into a bank account. Call it a trust fund.

You can build this trust from the moment your child is born by showing up for her when she needs you. Your baby needs you to help her feel safe, seen, soothed, and secure. By quickly, sensitively, and predictably responding to her, meeting her needs, and holding her,

You build your child's secure base from the very beginning.

you're giving her the best gift possible in terms of brain development and her ability to trust that she will be taken care of.

People used to believe that babies would be spoiled if they were held too much. Some experts have even taught that babies are capable of manipulating their parents. Fortunately, science has demonstrated otherwise. We now know that newborn children don't have the ability to manipulate. Manipulation, after all, is a very sophisticated skill that requires the prefrontal cortex to process complex thinking, and that part of the brain takes time to develop. Babies' needs are *needs,* not mere desires. It's not spoiling when we give our children what they need—when we comfort them when they're upset, feed them when they're hungry, hold them when they ask to be held, or help them sleep when they're tired. Paying attention to what your small child needs and giving it to him will allow you to feel more confident in your own instincts and in understanding what he's communicating to you. Sometimes, yes, a baby might be more "high need" (a phrase that's more helpful and accurate than "difficult" or "demanding" or "spoiled"), and in that case he simply may require more help from you to feel calm and safe and comforted. That's how you begin to build a secure base that will benefit both of you as he grows up—by tuning in, being present, and being there when he needs you.

A quick note to new parents: All that being said, you have needs too! It might help from time to time to get someone else to come over and nurture your baby for a while so you can sleep and shower or do something for yourself. And please take just an hour or two to go out to eat without your little one—preferably within the first six weeks of his life. This can make a huge difference in helping you feel like yourself again and to remind you that you matter, too. Remember, historically, we didn't raise our babies so isolated from support and help. In our evolutionary history and in many cultures around the world in the not-so-distant past, parenting was a responsibility shared with a select few other nonparent figures, something called alloparenting in the literature. Contemporary culture often doesn't support this important way we developed to raise children in community. So you may need to find those trusted individuals in your life—they could be your relatives or close friends or people in your neighborhood who are caregiving as well—and take a needed break. Care for yourself and replenish your energy and vitality. Chances are, after that break you'll actually be glad to come home and pay attention to your baby's needs once again.

As your child grows, you'll have a seemingly infinite number of chances to add to the trust fund. As a two-year-old at the park, she'll likely need you at some point because someone has taken her shovel or thrown a ball at her. When she comes to you in tears, you can offer a trust-building response. Based on how you yourself were parented, you might be tempted to say something dismissive like, "Don't cry, you're fine." As we said, some schools of thought argue that such a response will make your child stronger, tougher. ("They've gotta learn sometime!")

But there are a few problems with this logic. One has to do with timing. Yes, children have to learn at some point that the world can be a painful place. But they just learned that from the experience itself, and as the regulatory circuits of the brain are developing in the first three years, parental attunement to the internal experience is important to help them build the ability to regulate their own internal states. Plus, do they have to learn to face all the harsh realities of the world *as two-year-olds,* and on their own? Can't they be supported a little while longer? What's more, think about the message they receive when they are in distress, and their parent tells them (1) not to express their emotions because (2) they're really *not* in distress. That's a pretty powerful double whammy, to be told to hide your emotions as well as not to trust what you're feeling. They don't feel "fine," but you're telling them that they are, so they have to either distrust you or distrust their own experience.

We don't want to overstate this point. You're not going to ruin your child's emotional facility by telling her "Don't cry, you're fine." But if she hears that message over and over again when she's experi-

The Relational Trust Fund: Are you making
withdrawals or deposits?

Withdrawal

Deposit

encing big emotions and needs to be made to feel safe, it can significantly impact the way she views you and her internal world. And all
it takes is a slight shift in language to remind us about honoring our
children's experiences and to impact their perspective on the world

in a positive way. A powerful message you can give your kids when they're upset is, "You're safe. I'm here. You're not alone. It's going to be okay." Try this the next time your child runs to you, crying hard and afraid or upset about something. Feel her little body relax as her nervous system begins to understand that you've shown up for her, that she doesn't have to feel threatened and can instead feel safe and secure in your arms.

As your child gets older, into school-age and even teen years, your responses to her experiences will continue to shape her attachment relationship with you, and thus her perspective on relationships and the world. When she's left out of a social group, or doesn't get the part in the play, or experiences her first breakup, you will make a deposit in her trust fund every time she needs you and you show up. This is true not only for her individual experiences away from you, but also for what takes place between the two of you, as when she's failing to successfully navigate the disappointments and frustrations of every-day life and the boundaries you set. For instance, when she's com-pletely *devastated* that you're not serving the fried fish sticks she loved at her aunt's house, or she's angry that media time is up, or she's yelling that her brother is "the most annoying human who ever lived!"—these are also opportunities to build trust as we show up with empathy, while still honoring family rules and boundaries. You're making a deposit in the trust fund when you respond by say-ing, "That's so frustrating when your screen time is up and you're right in the middle of the level. I know that's hard. I get frustrated, too, when I have to interrupt something I'm working on." Again, you don't have to give in. Just show up. Doing so strengthens the relation-ship.

On the other hand, if you have trouble showing up, the amount of trust in the relationship will take a hit. We know a woman, Lee Ann, who told us about attending her first high-school party as a fourteen-year-old. An older friend who drove her to the party and was going to drive her home later ended up drinking alcohol that evening. Lee Ann called her parents to ask what she should do. She knew not to ride with someone who had been drinking. The parents, though, were hosting a party of their own, and when Lee Ann asked her mother's advice, she was told, "Is she still able to drive? If she hasn't had that much it should be fine." Lee Ann now says, "That was the moment I really *got* what I guess I'd always known. That I was on my own. That my parents weren't going to be there for me when I needed them."

As you might imagine, this wasn't the only time that Lee Ann's parents failed to show up for her. She has grown into an adult who is successful in many areas of her life, but she has also struggled in her marriage and is now having to go through the painful (but crucial) endeavor of earning the secure attachment her parents never gave her. Instead of building a secure base as a child with the help of parents who made her feel safe, she's now having to do so as an adult.

> We want to build the firm belief for our children that when they need us, we'll be there to support them, even when we can't—or choose not to—resolve the specific issue they're facing.

By now you know we're not saying that parents should step in and solve every problem their kids face. Instead, we're saying we want to build the firm belief for our children that when they need us, we'll be there to support them, even when we can't—or choose not to—resolve the specific issue they're facing. So watch for ways to make deposits into the relational trust fund. Each time you do so you'll be strengthening your child's secure base, meaning she can venture out on her own from a stable launching pad and develop even more confidence and independence.

Strategy #2 for Promoting a Secure Base: Teach Mindsight Skills

As we've said throughout the book and this chapter, one of a parent's primary goals is to provide such a deep experience with security that kids reach a point where they can find security for themselves. As our final strategy we want to give you a few examples of ways you can teach your children to show up for themselves when they need to feel more secure. In all of our books we stress the importance of empowering children in this way, because when we provide them with the gift of mindsight, where they better understand their own as well as another person's mind, we give them the opportunity to live lives full of meaning and significance, both as individuals and in relationships with others. Whether they use their mindsight to help themselves feel safe, understand and see the essence of who they truly are, or soothe themselves and return to the green zone when intense emotions crop up, these skills offer children (as well as adults) the means to further develop a deep-seated security that can be accessed at any time.

For example, using his mindsight skills, a child can take initiative and actually lessen the painful effects of difficult moments in life. One mom we know, Lucia, told us a story about how she taught mindsight skills to her son, Joey, just before he entered middle school. They had just come back from a trip to the beach, and Lucia had an idea of how to help Joey understand the concept. While they were playing in the surf together, Lucia had taught her son how to dive below waves rather than letting them hit him at full force. Joey had been delighted and amazed to learn how calm the water seemed beneath the surface, even when especially strong waves crashed overhead.

When they got home from the beach, Lucia explained to her son that waves are like events that come at us in life. Some are pleasant, some aren't. And just as Joey learned to duck beneath the violent ocean waves and find the calm beneath, he could do the same in a metaphorical sense when difficult events threatened to make life hard on him. He could watch for waves as they appeared, coming at him, and identify them. He could say, "Here comes a scary wave and I feel worried," or "This wave is kinda sad, and that's how I feel." Then he could visualize himself diving down below that wave and allowing it to pass overhead before rising to the surface again. Lucia taught him this kind of visualization, along with some other simple ways he could find calm within himself—get still and pay attention to his breathing; lie on his bed with one palm on his stomach and one on his heart; sit outside and focus on clouds moving across the sky while becoming calm within—and they practiced these techniques together.

She worked with Joey to help him understand that if at any point he felt anxiety or tension or fear or any other negative emotion, all he had to do was use these various mindsight skills to go within himself and find calm. Not to deny his feelings, but to keep them from taking over. He had access to these strategies any time he needed them, and they would help him dive beneath the waves threatening to overpower him, allowing him to find the peace and security within himself. As Lucia explained to Joey, "Under the water there, that's the real you. The waves are always going to come crashing in—sometimes in ways that are fun, and sometimes in ways that aren't. It's just like at the beach. Those waves are going to keep on rolling in toward the shore. But you have a choice: You don't have to have your inner calm self tossed around by waves of fear or sadness. The core you is that quiet place within yourself, and you can go there any time you want, whether you're happy or sad."

You can teach your kids similar mindsight skills, empowering them to use their mind to claim their security, even when you're not around. Like Joey, they can watch for dangerous or overwhelming or anxious or sad waves descending upon them, and instead of facing them head on and getting pummeled, they can dive down and find the calm within themselves.

Instead of getting pummeled by every emotional wave that comes their way...

Kids can learn to dive down and find the calm that lies beneath.

However, as Lucia said, the waves will keep coming, whether we know how to dive beneath them or not. Some will crash down on us, and crash hard, even when we do everything right. So as kids get older, we can expand the metaphor and make important points that require a bit more sophistication. For example, an important lesson we can teach our children is how to recognize the waves for what they are: temporary emotional events and *not* our core identity. They are experiences that occur *as part of* our lives. They aren't the essence or totality of who we are. Just because a child gets bullied and feels scared doesn't mean that he's a victim in every area of his life. Just because someone performs poorly on a test doesn't mean she's a bad student. Those are just emotional events in their lives, and they have nothing to do with a person's core identity, that calm place within.

When you teach your children mindsight skills that empower them to separate the events of their lives from their inner experience, you'll also be teaching them a key truth regarding emotions: that feelings are important and should definitely be recognized as such, but we also should recognize that they are flowing and changing throughout our lives, and throughout our day. We need to teach our kids to, yes, of course, pay attention to what they're feeling. Feelings reveal and give meaning to life. We never want to deny our emotions; it's important to be aware of what's happening within us. But we also want to teach them not to *over*react to their feelings. Learning to have presence as parents means creating a space inside of ourselves that allows us to be receptive to our child's feelings without becoming overwhelmed by them. With our own mindsight skills engaged, we can be a role model for how to be aware of feelings as real and important without being flooded by them. When our children see our openness to what they feel, they, too, can learn how to be receptive to their own inner states without being swept up by them. They learn from us that feelings can keep changing, like the waves and the tide. And as with the sea, we want to be mindful of what's happening so we're not flooded by rising waters, or knocked over by the waves.

When emotions are painful, teaching our children that even pain can be taken into awareness and be something to learn from is an important mindsight skill to convey. Kids can find it really powerful to learn that their pain doesn't last forever. Yes, emotional waves are going to come, and keep coming, but you can learn to surf them or dive underneath them. We want our children to understand how to savor the good moments and endure the painful ones, knowing all the while that emotions soon pass and transform into something else.

Dan was interviewed on the radio recently by a father who said that one busy day when he was impatient with his younger daughter, her sister came up to him and said that he "should try talking to her about her feelings, not telling her what to feel." When the dad asked this wise older daughter where she learned that, she said that she had read it in our book, *The Whole-Brain Child,* in the kids' section, which he had just purchased that weekend but hadn't read yet. (He has since read it.)

Children have a lot to teach *us,* too. Families that are open to reminding themselves to see the mind in each member provide the loving setting where everyone can become more present for their own inner lives and the lives of each person in the family. Mindsight enables us to remember, and be reminded, that respecting the subjective experiences of each member of a family cultivates the kind of emotional integration at the heart of secure attachment.

All of these lessons and the ways we cultivate security result from a few simple mindsight skills you can teach your kids. By helping them understand the wave and tide metaphor, learn to pay attention to their breath, and see the events of their lives as separate from their identity, you'll be giving them tools that will wire their brains to provide security *for themselves.* Of course they will still depend on you as well, but they'll know that when they need to find their inner resources that lead to security, they are always available.

Showing Up for Ourselves

How secure do you feel in your own life? In your relationships, do you have people who regularly help you feel safe, seen, and soothed, leading you to a deep and profound security? And, whether you do or not, how good are you at providing the Four S's for yourself, the way we've been discussing helping our kids learn to do?

We've found that many caring adults who are really good at helping the people around them feel safe, seen, soothed, and secure aren't always so good at befriending and taking care of themselves.

"What do I need right now?" isn't a question they typically ask themselves, choosing instead to take care of others, even to their own detriment. Slow down right now and take some time to be quiet with the following questions, which ask you to consider your overall experiences with security when you were a child, as well as how good you are as an adult when it comes to providing yourself with the care and compassion you need, then offering the same to your kids.

1. How secure did you feel as a child?

2. Which one of the first three S's did your parents do best at providing for you?

3. Where could they have done better? Do you wish you had been kept more safe? Been seen or soothed more?

4. Did they help you develop the ability to find security within yourself, without having to rely only on others? Or were you left to do that on your own?

5. What could you do at this stage in your life to do a better job of showing up for yourself? How could you provide yourself with more security by showering yourself with the Four S's?

6. What about your kids? Have they developed the security that comes from feeling consistently safe, seen, and soothed when they need it? How do you feel about how well you've responded to their needs quickly, sensitively, and predictably?

7. Are you finding ways to help them build skills for developing their own inner security, even when you're not around? How

are you as a secure base? As a solid and supportive launching pad?

8. What's one thing you can do right now, today, to help your children feel more secure than they already do? It might have to do with helping them feel more safe. Or maybe you feel like you've been riding them too much about grades, or achievement, or your own expectations, and they haven't felt seen and embraced for who they are. Or is there something they're going through where you could help them just by being nearby and offering a soothing presence? Small steps toward security can make a huge difference.

From the Playground to the Dorm Room
A Look into the Future

Imagine a moment that seems far down the road, but that, we assure you, will be here before you know it. Your adorable child has grown into adolescence and is now a college freshman. Can you picture it? Try it right now, just as a thought experiment. What will your child look like in the not-distant-at-all future? Will he be tall? Will he be wearing glasses? What color hair? Now picture yourself hugging him goodbye and tearfully climbing back into your car.

As you drive away from the dorm, you think about what kind of person your child has become. Have you provided a secure base? How will he feel as he launches into this new and exciting and, yes, scary phase of life? Imagine that you have reliably helped him feel safe, seen, and soothed throughout his young life, and by the time he is eighteen he has developed the security to find that same support from within. He still needs you plenty and has lots to learn along the way, but by this time he knows how to access the Four S's when needed—both by reaching out to others and by relying on his inner resources.

In terms of safety, this means young adults must make good decisions regarding driving, alcohol, sexual activity, and all the other important concerns parents have. But it also means keeping themselves safe when it comes to relationships and how they take care of themselves. The hope is that they will have developed the inner compass to draw personal boundaries and make wise choices, regardless of what someone else or a crowd might be pushing them to do.

As for being seen, they will have developed the capacity for personal insight. You will have spent years and years showing up for them, observing, demonstrating interest in, and responding with respect to what you notice is going on in their inner world. As a result, they will themselves have learned to pay attention to that world. They'll be aware of how they feel in a given situation, and they'll be able to recognize the moments when they begin to, say, enter the red zone of chaos. In response they will be able to regulate themselves emotionally and respond from their upstairs brain, rather than letting the downstairs brain take over. Likewise, they'll be able to pay attention to times when they feel tempted to play the victim role rather than making conscious choices to leave or alter a situation they don't feel good about. Simply by watching what's going on within themselves, and paying attention to their inner life, as you will have taught them to do over the years, they'll be able to feel seen and understood, and they'll likely choose friends and romantic partners where this trait is a mutual and understood part of the relationship.

They'll also know how to soothe themselves when facing the difficult moments of being away from home. As a child they will have seen you respond to their literal and figurative bruises by offering your P-E-A-C-E (your presence, engagement, affection, calm, and empathy) whenever they were hurting. They will have experienced that kind of inter-soothing and know its importance in a relationship, and they'll know how to provide themselves the necessary inner soothing when they feel homesick, experience heartache, face fears and uncertainties, and undergo any of the other challenges that come with gaining this new level of independence.

In short, they will launch into their new world from the secure base you've spent years helping them develop. Just as they did when they fearfully wandered away from you on the playground, increasingly widening the circle of security because they knew you were there watching, they will do the same in this significant moment of their life. And just as when they were children, they'll be confident that you'll show up when they need you, providing a safe haven to return to. They'll still make plenty of mistakes, and they'll experience their share of pain, but they'll do so from a place of security. You've helped them construct that internal working model of security that will last a lifetime. They'll attend their first classes, meet new friends, and explore a new campus with the certainty of knowing that when they reach out to you and need you to show up, that's just what you'll do—just as you've been doing for their whole lives. And they'll know that they can find others in their lives who can also become healthy, secure attachment figures—as friends, mentors, or romantic partners. That's healthy interdependence.

This vision of your securely attached eighteen-year-old originates now, today, no matter how young your child is. Parents who focus their attention on the inner experience of their children and perceive, make sense of, and respond respectfully to that mental life offer their kids the immeasurable gift of secure attachment. When we attune in this way, when we pay close attention to them and their internal landscape, they feel seen, they can be soothed, and in turn, they feel emotionally safe, developing both a sense of trust and a mental model of security.

The science confirms that this security doesn't require that you're perfect. You're not going to provide flawless care in every interaction you have with your child. But by repeatedly showing up—reliably making repairs when the inevitable ruptures occur—and providing the Four S's, you will be creating the kind of future that allows your child to flourish and thrive, even in the midst of life's harsh realities, as a young adult and throughout their whole life.

What we hope we've made clear here is that you can create this kind of future for your children, no matter what happened in your own past. History is not destiny. Research robustly reveals that no matter what happened to us, if we take the time to make sense of how the past has shaped our development, we can then free ourselves to become the kind of person and parent we want to be. This science of attachment is tremendously hopeful, confirming again and again that we can offer secure attachment to our kids regardless of how we ourselves were parented.

The science is tremendously hopeful, confirming again and again that we can offer secure attachment to our kids regardless of how we ourselves were parented.

What's more, we can earn secure attachment in our own lives, simply by doing the hard work of reflecting on the past and making sense of our past experiences. When we can tell a coherent story about where we've come from and how it affects us in the present, we can then take clear and powerful steps toward becoming the kind of parents we want to be.

What a magnificent time to be raising children with the knowledge we now have about how to shape the growth of strong connections in their brains and bodies. We hope that the ideas we've presented here have convinced you that showing up is the best gift you can give your children, because you will help them develop the inner resources and interpersonal skills that will cultivate long-lasting resilience and empower them to live full, connected, and meaningful lives. In many ways, learning to show up for our kids teaches them the skills of showing up fully for life itself. What better gift could we possibly offer?

REFRIGERATOR SHEET

The Power of Showing Up

By Daniel J. Siegel, M.D., and Tina Payne Bryson, Ph.D.

Children who form secure attachments with their caregivers lead happier and more fulfilling lives. These bonds are formed when parents respond to the needs of their children by providing the Four S's:

- **Safe:** Parents have two primary jobs when it comes to *KEEPING* kids safe, and making them *FEEL* safe: protect them from harm, and avoid becoming a source of fear and threat.

- **STRATEGIES FOR PROMOTING SAFETY:**

  ◉ *First, do no harm:* Make a commitment that you won't be the source of fear in your home.
  ◉ *Repair, repair, repair!* When there's a breach in your relationship with your child, reconnect as soon as possible and apologize if necessary.
  ◉ *Help your kids feel snug in a safe harbor:* Create within your home an overall environment of safety and well-being.

- **Seen:** Truly seeing our kids is about three main things: (1) attuning to their internal mental state on a profound and meaningful level; (2) coming to understand their inner life; and (3) responding to what we see in a timely and effective manner. This three-step process helps children "feel felt."

- **STRATEGIES FOR HELPING YOUR KIDS FEEL SEEN:**

  ◉ *Let your curiosity lead you to take a deeper dive:* Simply observe your kids. Take the time to look and really understand what's going on with them, discarding preconceived ideas and avoiding snap judgments.
  ◉ *Make space and time to look and learn:* Generate opportunities

that allow your kids to show you who they are. Create space for conversations that take you more fully into their world so you can learn more about them and see details you might otherwise miss.

- **Soothed:** When a child is in a state of internal distress, that negative experience can be shifted by an interaction with a caregiver who attunes to and cares for her. She might still suffer, but at least she won't be alone in her pain. Based on this parent-directed "inter-soothing," she'll learn to provide "inner soothing" for herself.

- **STRATEGIES TO PROMOTE INNER SELF-SOOTHING:**
  - *Build a calming internal toolkit: Before* emotional situations arise, work with your child to develop simple tools and strategies to help him calm himself.
  - *Offer your P-E-A-C-E:* When your kids are upset, give them your presence, engagement, affection, calm, and empathy.

- **Secure:** The fourth "S" results from the first three. We give our kids a secure base when we show them that they are safe, that there's someone who sees them and cares for them intimately, and that we will soothe them in distress. They then learn to keep THEMSELVES safe, to see THEMSELVES as worthy, to soothe THEMSELVES when things go wrong.

- **STRATEGIES TO PROMOTE A SECURE BASE:**
  - *Invest in a relational trust fund:* Each time your kids need you and you show up, the trust in the relationship increases. You make a deposit in the relational trust fund.
  - *Teach mindsight skills:* Teach your children to show up for themselves when they need to feel more secure. Provide them with the gift of mindsight, which helps them better understand their own as well as another person's mind. With mindsight skills they can live lives full of security, meaning, and significance, both as individuals and in relationships with others.

ACKNOWLEDGMENTS

Writing together is a joy, and Tina and Dan wish to express our gratitude for each other, and our teammates, Scott Bryson and Caroline Welch. Together, the four of us have the fun of combining our professional passions with brainstorming ideas from our lives together as parents raising our collective five children now ranging from early adolescence to early adulthood.

We'd also like to acknowledge Marnie Cochran and the team at Ballantine/Penguin Random House and the wonderful assembly of copy editors and marketing professionals who work to help get the ideas of this work out into the world in as clear and concise a manner as possible. Thank you for all the collaborative sessions to bring this work into the world!

Doug Abrams and his team at Idea Architects have been a pleasure to collaborate with, working with us from the beginning in finding the proper literary home for this integrative approach to parenting. Thanks, Doug, for the fun and laughter along the way. What a joy!

We applaud our respective teams at The Mindsight Institute, The Center for Connection, and The Play Strong Institute for all the ways they work with us to impact minds, brains, and relationships. A big thanks to our teams for helping us share the science of connection and healing in the world.

We both work closely with parents, children, educators, and mental health professionals from a range of fields in trying to bring interpersonal neurobiology into practical use in homes, classrooms, and clinical consulting suites. While we ourselves teach to many, it is our honor to be the learners in those educational conversations, soaking in the questions and the wisdom of therapists, clients, teachers, parents, and kids that help us continually open our mind to imagine new ways of synthesizing science for practical ways to help people grow strong and bring well-being into their individual and relational lives. We have deep gratitude for our parents and extended family who have nurtured us and encouraged us along the way.

Finally, we'd like to thank our respective children: Ben, Luke, and JP; and Alex and Maddi, for being our primary teachers in learning how we can tap into the power of showing up in our lives together. We love you and are so grateful for the gift of our relationships!

ABOUT THE AUTHORS

Daniel J. Siegel, M.D., is a physician; child, adolescent, and adult psychiatrist; and clinical professor at the David Geffen UCLA School of Medicine. He has been responsible for the publication of dozens of books as author, coauthor, or editor, including authoring *Brainstorm: The Power and Purpose of the Teenage Brain; Mindsight: The New Science of Personal Transformation; Mind: A Journey to the Heart of Being Human; Aware: The Science and Practice of Presence;* and *The Developing Mind: How Relationships and the Brain Interact to Shape Who We Are.* He is the executive director of the Mindsight Institute, an educational center for interpersonal neurobiology that combines wide-ranging fields of science into one framework for understanding human development and the nature of well-being. He lectures throughout the world, online, and in person for parents, professionals, and the public. You can reach him at DrDanSiegel .com.

Facebook.com/DrDanSiegel

Twitter: @DrDanSiegel

Instagram: @drdansiegel

Tina Payne Bryson, Ph.D., is the founder and executive director of The Center for Connection, a multidisciplinary clinical practice, and of The Play Strong Institute, a center devoted to the study, research, and practice of play therapy through a neurodevelopmental and relational lens. She is a licensed clinical social worker, providing pediatric and adolescent psychotherapy and parenting consultations. She keynotes conferences and conducts workshops for parents, educators, clinicians, and industry leaders around the world. She earned her Ph.D. from the University of Southern California and lives in Los Angeles with her husband and three children. You can reach her at TinaBryson .com.

Facebook.com/TinaPayneBrysonPhd

Twitter: @tinabryson

Instagram: @tinapaynebryson

ABOUT THE TYPE

This book was set in Minion, a 1990 Adobe Originals typeface by Robert Slimbach (b. 1956). Minion is inspired by classical, old-style typefaces of the late Renaissance, a period of elegant, beautiful, and highly readable type designs. Created primarily for text setting, Minion combines the aesthetic and functional qualities that make text type highly readable with the versatility of digital technology.